"Using the Emmaus-road story as th̲ his readers to walk alongside him ̲ struggles of his own walk with God. A testimony, I found myself enfolded w̲ Christ and inspired to face the next stage of my own journey with renewed hope and courage."

—**JOSHUA T. SEARLE**, Spurgeon's College

"In this very remarkable piece of theological autobiography, John Weaver remarks that 'by writing we impose a shape on the world.' He is surely speaking of this book, which is nothing less than his own spiritual journal. Through it he is giving shape to his own life, interpreting it theologically—but he is also encouraging every reader to do the same."

—**PAUL S. FIDDES**, University of Oxford

"John Weaver's book is refreshingly honest and helpful for insights gleaned from significant encounters in his life and offers practical applications to others alert to the pilgrimage of their lives. The bonus for me was the level of personal sharing of the author's life, spiritual encounters, and challenges. It is refreshing to receive these insights."

—**JAMES A. SMITH**, global mission
leader, Cooperative Baptist Fellowship

"John Weaver has woven together a rich tapestry of story, scholarship, and searing honesty, helping us to live our whole lives in God. Faithfully biblical, rooted in real life, wisely reflecting on experience, drawing on insights from events and people, John encourages us to fully inhabit our storied lives—alive, alert, fizzing with hope and grace. A real joy to read."

—**SIAN MURRAY-WILLIAMS**, moderator, Ministerial
Recognition Committee, the Baptist Union of Great Britain

"This book is an inspiration for reflective living. Using the Emmaus story, John helps us to see how reflection over the long journey of our lives may open our eyes to the presence of the risen Christ in the everyday. John's gift is to connect with the experience of disillusionment and uncertainty. Through deep reflection on his own story, he testifies to the saving hope that can be found on the darkest of roads."

—**MIKE PEARS**, director, IBTS, Amsterdam

Emmaus

Peter,
With my very best wishes and prayers
for your continuing journey
into Christ

August 2022

Emmaus

Journeying toward and onward from Emmaus

John Weaver

Foreword by Paul S. Fiddes

WIPF *&* STOCK · Eugene, Oregon

EMMAUS
Journeying toward and onward from Emmaus

Wipf & Stock
An Imprint of Wipf and Stock Publishers
199 W. 8th Ave., Suite 3
Eugene, OR 97401

www.wipfandstock.com

PAPERBACK ISBN: 978-1-6667-4370-8
HARDCOVER ISBN: 978-1-6667-4371-5
EBOOK ISBN: 978-1-6667-4372-2

07/12/22

for Sheila, my companion throughout life's journey

Contents

Foreword

by Paul S. Fiddes

JAMES WM. MCCLENDON, A Baptist theologian like our author, urged the writing of "biography as theology."[1] His proposal was to use biographical narrative in order to create "a theology of life," rather than just using biography to set out models of exemplary living to inspire the faithful. Attempts to follow his lead have often ended up with more biography than theology, losing theological reflection in recording the fine detail of incidents and events. In John Weaver's piece of *autobiography* as theology there is no such loss. He gives us just enough of his life's story to enable us to share imaginatively in his journey, and to engage in his practical theology. He tells us that he always advised his students who were attempting to reflect theologically on praxis to ask "what is God *doing* in what is happening here?" and he has clearly followed his own counsel.

John's approach to integrating autobiography and theology is to meditate on the story of the Emmaus road, when the risen Jesus met, accompanied and revealed himself to disillusioned disciples. He tells us that we can read the story from two perspectives: from that of the disciples and that of Christ himself. Together they give us a pattern for mission. But in this book he also weaves in another

1. McClendon, *Biography.*

perspective—his own life's journey. He himself has been, and still is, a disciple travelling to and from Emmaus. This rich threefold hermeneutic enables him to develop an appeal for a culture shift in the church. It is high time, he urges, to realise that journeying with Christ means forming a church and communicating a gospel that is relevant to the actual everyday life that people are leading today. Filling out McClendon's phrase "a theology of life" he writes about "whole-life church," "whole-life discipleship," and "whole-life mission." He has warning words about congregations that are success-driven, individualistic, and consumerist. He tells us that these are the convictions that grip him at the stage in life to which he has come, and I suggest that we would do well to pay attention to him. For the reader of this book will sense the authority with which he speaks, coming from many years of Christian ministry.

His stage of life is, he tells us, one of retirement and aging. He even refers to his situation in his mid-seventies, in a football analogy, as "playing in extra time." But what the reader should notice is that John's reflections on growing older do not appear at the end of the book, as one might expect with a mere autobiography. They appear exactly halfway through, and they are followed by a chapter which is about journeying away or "onward" from Emmaus. This is not an autobiography, but autobiographical *theology*. The remainder of the book continues to explore what it means to walk the journey of life with Christ, constantly developing in an understanding of where and how God is at work, often in surprising places. It is about being continually open to God and to oneself, learning to be vulnerable in our journey with others, and finding the companionship of a vulnerable God who shares human suffering. So as John gives an account of joining in the dance of the triune God, participating in God's own desire for a different world, it is clear that he sees his present stage of life as full of new opportunities to "journey into God," who "restores, redeems and renews." Aging, he tells us, is a movement onwards "into a broader and deeper world."

In encouraging us to write journals, John remarks that "by writing we impose a shape on the world." He is surely speaking of this book, which is nothing less than his own spiritual journal.

Through it he is giving shape to his own life, interpreting it theologically—that is from the perspective of asking, "where is God at work here?"—but he is also encouraging every reader to do the same. He speaks of the Christian community as a place where people share their stories, and interact with each other in interpreting experience, sharing "struggles, hopes, dreams, sorrow, mistakes, and pain."

I have in fact been privileged to share personally quite a lot of John's own story over the past four decades, as a friend and colleague in theological education and in the life of the Baptist family of churches worldwide. I have deeply appreciated sharing at least some of John's walk to Emmaus and onwards. I know that there is a great deal more to this story than the following pages disclose to us: John's ministry has been much more extensive, his thought (especially in the area of science and religion) has been more influential, and his impact on the lives of others more powerful, than he chooses modestly to reveal here. Much of what he does tell us about his career and publications is allowed to slip in almost casually between the lines. But then this is biography as *theology*, as talking about God, not as self-esteem. The reader is given, in this relatively brief span of pages, the very heart of John's thinking about church, mission, the kingdom of God, and the doing of theology that generations of students have valued hearing over the years.

It is significant that John quotes from another mutual friend, Karen Smith, on the theme of spirituality. She stresses that Christian spirituality develops as we examine our beliefs in the light of our experience of relationship with God, with others and with the wider world. We have John's exercise in doing this in our hands, in the shape of his story. But John records Karen as concluding that "story-telling, of course, is not simply a matter of relating an event—it is about seeking after truth that is beyond the story itself." The achievement of this book of autobiography as theology is that on every page it goes "beyond the story" to draw us into the truth that is personal and—ultimately—into Christ himself.

Preface

I TRUST THAT THE reader will find this text to be a witness of God's grace.

In essence it represents my journey toward, and onward from, Emmaus (Luke 24:13–35), and reflects the ways in which God has called and equipped me in life. It is in part autobiographical and in part reflective teaching as it covers my experience and witness, theological reflection, and proclamation.

It follows my life through my understanding and experience of God's grace: seeing God in others and in creation; learning about God through church, scientific discovery, and theological education; preaching and pastoring; and teaching and theological reflection.

As this book is about my discipleship, it focuses on experience, reflection, and sharing the truths I have learned both through Bible study and through the dialogue between science and faith. It is my faith story, which asks questions about how God acts in the world and in human lives; reflects on the nature of God and on God's desire for every human life; and on sharing the good news of new possibilities for a life in Christ, a life in all the fullness that

God has purposed, where the Christ who accompanies us on the road is able to make sense of our experiences.

So it follows that this book is composed of testimony, theological reflection, teaching, and preaching as it is an account of how I have experienced God's grace and calling on my life.

Along the way I have slowly come to understand who I am before God. I am strengthened by the revelation of God in Christ as expressed in Heb 1:1–4 and 4:14–16. The writer of this letter tells us that Jesus was tempted in every way that we are, yet did not give in to temptation, and that we can approach God through Christ.

> Therefore, since we have a great high priest who has ascended into heaven, Jesus the Son of God, let us hold firmly to the faith we profess. For we do not have a high priest who is unable to empathize with our weaknesses, but we have one who has been tempted in every way, just as we are—yet he did not sin. Let us then approach God's throne of grace with confidence, so that we may receive mercy and find grace to help us in our time of need. (Heb 4: 14–16)

In chapter 1 he tells us that Jesus Christ is the agent of creation, he is the revelation of God's glory, he is the perfect revelation—he is truly God and truly human. So our writer is observing that this God knows me in the humanity of Christ; he knows my life and understands what it means to be me. This is good news for all of us. The creator of the universe is not some distant uninterested power, but in Jesus understands what makes me tick, what makes me laugh, what makes me cry, and accepts me for who I am.

At a college retreat in South Wales at the beginning of this century those of us who gathered together were each invited to reflect on how we understood ourselves and God. The following is a prayer that I wrote:

Preface

Here I am Lord:
fractured
flawed
failing

. . . but in Christ I am:
redeemed
restored
renewed

. . . and through the Spirit I am:
brought into a relationship
being transformed
becoming truly human

. . . hear my thanksgiving:
God my creator
Christ my saviour
Holy Spirit my companion

. . . for you are the eternal God:
watching
waiting
within and without

. . . my friend, my Saviour and risen Lord:
now
and forever
Amen.[1]

1. First published in Jump and Weaver, *Love:Work,* 12.

Acknowledgements

I AM INDEBTED TO the many people who I have encountered, and who have accompanied me, on the journey of faith. I want to pick out some—though not all, the number would be too great—who have played a significant part in my experience of God and the ways in which God works in the world and in human lives, especially in my life.

There were my parents, loving Christians who taught me so much about the faith, and especially how that faith should be lived as a disciple of Christ. There is my wife, Sheila, who I met in church, while at University in Swansea. She has been my life partner for over fifty years, and together we have shared and grown through many experiences of the presence of God.

Moving beyond family, Professor Dick Owen, a renowned expert on the geology of the South Wales Coalfield, was my teacher and the supervisor for my PhD. He was insightful and caring, great fun to be with, and a witness to his own personal faith through his ministry as a Methodist lay-preacher.

In Derbyshire during my first employment as a lecturer in geology, our minister Peter Grange was both a channel of God's blessing, and a minister of God's revelation and challenge for my

Christian life. It was here that we made life-long Christian friends and companions on the road of faith: Peter and his wife Janet, David and Margaret Hughes, and Jeanette and David Turner.

In theological college in Oxford my tutors Barrie White, Rex Mason, John Morgan Wynne, and Paul Fiddes opened my eyes to biblical truth and the commitment to Christian ministry.

In my first pastorate in Rushden the members of the church diaconate were both a support and those who kept my feet firmly on the ground of real and relevant ministry. Amongst these I hold David Hunt in high regard for his faith and wise counsel.

Through my teaching appointments in Oxford and Cardiff I gained a great deal from each of the three hundred-plus Baptist and Anglican students that I sought to prepare for ministry. It is a great joy to see the ways in which God has used many of them in ministry.

Some of my colleagues in these academic settings have been special companions through their witness, knowledge and love. I mention a few of these who shaped my ongoing life and witness: Alan and Ellie Kreider who taught me about hospitality, humility, and integrity; Paul Fiddes and Keith Ward who encouraged my exploration of the dialogue between science and faith; and Stephen Pattison and Simon Woodman who challenged my thinking about the relevance of doctrine and Scripture for our contemporary world. Finally it was the late R.T. "Dick" France, a colleague of mine in Oxford and external examiner of courses I taught at Cardiff University, who encouraged me to write this book in my retirement; and John Rackley with whom I have spent many hours in discussion about the subject matter of this text. I am also indebted to conversations with David Kerrigan, Sîan Murray-Williams, and Joshua Searle.

Introduction

I HAD BEEN WITH a couple in the local hospital as they came to the decision to turn off the life support for their daughter/step daughter who had been involved in a serious car crash. The next day I was called to their home, where grief had overtaken them, especially the mother. On my way to the house I prayed continually that God would give me the right words to say or not say. I received God's gracious though perplexing answer—over and over again, almost audible in my car: "Tell her I love her." This couple were living together, both had left their former spouses some months earlier, and now this tragedy had occurred.

I got to the house and sat with the family, sharing their grief, listening to their pain and questions about why this had happened to them and what were they to do next. Throughout the hour or more that I spent with them I kept hearing God's word to me, "Tell her I love her." Eventually I spoke to the child's mother as I believe that God had instructed me. I said, I don't know if this is going to help you, but I believe that God wants to say to you: "I love you." It was as if a dam had burst, the tears flowed and she shook for some minutes, eventually saying, "Those are just the words I needed to hear." "I thought that God was punishing me for my adultery by taking my child from me."

We spoke about God's love and the truth that God does not act in such a way. Pain and grief are part of life, but God does not bring such pain as a punishment. We continued to speak of the gospel message of forgiveness and God's love with all the possibilities for life beyond their current situation of loss. Some months after the funeral the couple were married, inviting God to be part of their ongoing life together. Yet I am sure that the pain, grief and guilt continued.

The Emmaus road is one of those biblical stories that speaks to us about Jesus sharing our journey and making sense of our deepest needs and feelings. Jesus presents us with an example of how we might walk with others we meet in life.

This is one of the most familiar Easter resurrection stories. It is often recounted at Eucharistic services where the Lord's Supper is celebrated; Jesus revealed in the breaking of the bread. The experience of Cleopas and his wife of their "hearts burning within them" is like that recorded by John Wesley concerning his spiritual conversion on May 24th, 1738 at a meeting in Aldersgate. Wesley recalls that someone read from Luther's *Preface to the Epistle to Romans*. About 8:45 p.m. "while he was describing the change which God works in the heart through faith in Christ, I felt my heart strangely warmed. I felt I did trust in Christ, Christ alone for salvation; and an assurance was given me that He had taken away my sins, even mine, and saved me from the law of sin and death."[1]

We can read the story of Cleopas and his wife as recorded by Luke (Luke 24:13–35), here as translated by Eugene Peterson:

> **13-16** That same day two of them were walking to the village Emmaus, about seven miles out of Jerusalem. They were deep in conversation, going over all these things that had happened. In the middle of their talk and questions, Jesus came up and walked along with them. But they were not able to recognize who he was. **17-18** He asked, "What's this you're discussing so intently as you walk along?" They just stood there, long-faced, like they had lost their best friend. Then one of them, his name

---

1 Wesley, *Works of John Wesley*, 18:249–50.

was Cleopas, said, "Are you the only one in Jerusalem who hasn't heard what's happened during the last few days?" **19-24** He said, "What has happened?" They said, "The things that happened to Jesus the Nazarene. He was a man of God, a prophet, dynamic in work and word, blessed by both God and all the people. Then our high priests and leaders betrayed him, got him sentenced to death, and crucified him. And we had our hopes up that he was the One, the One about to deliver Israel. And it is now the third day since it happened. But now some of our women have completely confused us. Early this morning they were at the tomb and couldn't find his body. They came back with the story that they had seen a vision of angels who said he was alive. Some of our friends went off to the tomb to check and found it empty just as the women said, but they didn't see Jesus." **25-27** Then he said to them, "So thick-headed! So slow-hearted! Why can't you simply believe all that the prophets said? Don't you see that these things had to happen, that the Messiah had to suffer and only then enter into his glory?" Then he started at the beginning, with the Books of Moses, and went on through all the Prophets, pointing out everything in the Scriptures that referred to him.

28-31 They came to the edge of the village where they were headed. He acted as if he were going on but they pressed him: "Stay and have supper with us. It's nearly evening; the day is done." So he went in with them. And here is what happened: He sat down at the table with them. Taking the bread, he blessed and broke and gave it to them. At that moment, open-eyed, wide-eyed, they recognized him. And then he disappeared.

32 Back and forth they talked. "Didn't we feel on fire as he conversed with us on the road, as he opened up the Scriptures for us?" **33-34** They didn't waste a minute. They were up and on their way back to Jerusalem. They found the Eleven and their friends gathered together, talking away: "It's really happened! The Master has been raised up—Simon saw him!" **35** Then the two went over everything that happened on the road and how they recognized him when he broke the bread.[2]

In this passage we find an encounter, an education, an encouragement, and an evangelistic and pastoral pattern. We are encountered by Jesus, educated in the meaning of Scripture, encouraged to know the resurrection presence of Jesus, and given an example of how to help others to life in all its fullness through walking beside them along life's road.

In early retirement it is possible to take a more detached view of how the churches attempt to witness to the gospel. We can reflect on what we see, retrace our own tracks through life and dare to think that we may have something to offer of wisdom, perspective, and experience. The story of Jesus joining the two disciples leaving Jerusalem for Emmaus on the first Easter evening has been a deeply important text for me. The center of my faith journey is based on an ongoing relationship with the Christian scriptures, and in my personal encounters with the risen Lord Jesus. For me the scriptures contain the pathways of God's grace in the life of the Jewish people, the particular characters and communities in that story, which culminate in Jesus and his own followers. The Emmaus road experience is more than a story of what happened once upon a time. It is blueprint of what being a follower of the post-resurrection Christ means.

Jesus never forces his ways on us. Look at some of his encounters with people: blind Bartimaeus (Mark 10:46–52) "What do you want me to do for you?"; the two blind men on the road from Jericho to Jerusalem (Matt 20:29–34) "What do you want me to do for you?"; the man at the pool of Bethesda (John 5:1–15) "Do you want to get well?"; to the woman in the temple accused of adultery (John 8:1–11) "Woman, where are they? Has no one condemned you?"; and now on the road to Emmaus on this first Easter evening (Luke 24:13–35) "What are you discussing together as you walk along?" Tell me about it; what's your story?

2. Peterson, *Message*.

In our fellowship life together, and in our part in the mission of Christ, we might learn from Jesus' way of dealing with people, his interest in them, his understanding of their way of life. First of all, Jesus gets alongside and listens. He then asks them to tell their own story, which they do including all their dashed hopes. Then Jesus begins to explore their story in the light of the Scriptures and the promises concerning the Messiah. Finally, he sits down to meal with them, where they recognize him and respond by returning to Jerusalem to share what they have learnt with the rest of the disciples.

What stories will our friends and neighbours tell? And what are their questions and observations of the world in which we all live? Our own society has changed and the church is no longer at the center. We need help in a new situation. The church in the UK is generally in decline. Churchgoing across all denominations in England is predicted to fall from about three million today to about seven hundred thousand within forty years.

Some churches are heavily involved in community projects and care of the disadvantaged. This is a contribution that is increasingly recognized by local and national government and they encourage and support churches to be involved in community projects. There is much happening at the local level with food banks, debt counseling, housing grants, with such organisations as Christians Against Poverty and involvement with non-church groups such as Citizens UK.

There are three important questions about our engagement with the society we seek to serve:

- Does our church effectively help us to live in the contemporary world? To engage faith and life/work issues.

- Is our church effective in preparing people for their role in mission? To understand the current context and to experience the power and presence of God.

- Is our church an attractive community to those who don't know Jesus? Do we present Jesus—for example, are we a demonstration of Christ-like love.

If we all live in the world, why is the church alien to those with whom we live the rest of the week? The answer may be that we have created a church culture that is not authentic for the way in which we live, let alone for those outside the church. Statistics show 47 percent of Christians say that church teaching is irrelevant to their daily lives. The problem is not of form but of content. Many churchgoers are not looking to be entertained but to find wisdom for living.

We need a reality and integrity in all we do and say. Christianity that is relevant to daily living will be honest, open, vulnerable. It does not censor the agony of broken relationships, the bewilderment of unanswered questions, the struggle of work, the scandal of death, the impact of evil on ourselves and those around us. Too often the church looks to be life denying rather than life affirming. We have emphasized a sacred-secular divide, which our Christian forebears would not have recognised. We believe that some parts of our life are not really important to God—work, school, sport, TV, politics, sex—but anything to do with prayers, church services and church-based activity is. Many people have never heard a sermon on the theology of work; the God-given joy of sexual relationships within marriage; our political responsibility; or how to challenge the many opinions produced by the media.

The late John Smith, leader of the Labour Party in the early 1990s, coined the phrase "the me generation" to describe UK society at the time. We might ask: do we limit our Christian faith to "me" and "my God" or do we work out our Christian faith in joining Christ's transforming mission in the world?

North American church leader and evangelist Brian McLaren asks: If Jesus is going to change the world, what sort of community will his followers have to be?[3] Not an institutional church fussing over its organization and doctrine, but something much more radical, rampant, risk-taking. The central "missional" argument of Scripture is that we are called out of the world to be an alternative humanity in the midst of the nations and cultures of the world—a redeemed, renewed, transformed community who stand as a prophetic witness to how God intended creation to be. Our prophetic

3. McLaren, *Everything Must Change*, 52–58.

task is to build communities that will survive within a suicidal world, where making money is the driving force. It is the dream of having money to be happy. But there isn't enough for everyone and so there will be jealousy and violence. So, as the "haves" of society, our desired lifestyle needs to be protected. We employ police, security firms and surveillance, for which we need personnel at a significant cost.

A glance at the opening chapters of Ecclesiastes, where the wisdom writer engages in conversation with his culture puts all this in perspective (Eccl 1:12—2:14). Written twenty-five hundred years ago this passage speaks directly into our own world and our experience of life. The philosopher probes our way of life as he seeks to find if there is anything of lasting value. We live in a society that is preoccupied with human achievements good, bad, and indifferent; with possessions; and with insatiable demands for pleasure and satisfaction. There are many rivals to Christianity, not so much in the other world religions, but rather in the materialism, individualism, and the do-it-yourself religion of New Age myth and fantasy. Money, sex and power; knowledge, pleasure and achievement. The philosopher puts himself in the place of Solomon; he chooses Solomon because of Solomon's reputation for wisdom and for wealth. As a second Solomon, he has the resources for his experimental search for satisfaction in life. But with devastating honesty the philosopher is quick to tell us the worst, the experimental search has come to nothing. People dash down various blind alleys in life, finding the answers to all the world's mysteries: the intellectual's blind alley; the pleasure seeker's blind alley, wine, women, and song; and the workaholic's blind alley of human achievement. Mind, body, and energy ultimately end up nowhere but the grave, says the philosopher, which makes them all about as substantial as candyfloss, even while you enjoy them.

Finding satisfaction and contentment is one conversation we might have with our neighbors. It is in Christ that we find value, love, and purpose, someone who makes sense of life and who can hold on to us in the nighttime of fear and anxiety. We are the gathered church at worship on Sundays and in our mid-week fellowship groups in order to be strengthened to be the scattered church during the rest of the week. It is as the church scattered that we are involved in the mission of Christ.

Although, of course, we can't protect ourselves from the panic of the money markets; and it is impossible to protect ourselves from random acts of violence; and even when we have our wealth and security it is no guarantee of happiness. We are in a suicidal tail spin in which we can act, but we don't. For example, considering global climate change, the late Sir John Houghton maintained that we have the understanding to address the environmental problem but we do not have the will. He observes that our lack of will is a function of human sin.

The gospel is about saving and transforming the people of God to function as an alternative community in which the justice and compassion and creativity of God are demonstrated. By its very existence such a community will challenge the corrupting systems and hierarchies of the world and will demonstrate that things can be different. It will maintain the hope that sin and death will not have the last word in the life of our community.

1

Journeying toward Emmaus

So, what is Luke telling us? What was going on?

There are numerous commentators who have explored the journey of the two disciples from Jerusalem to Emmaus on Easter Day as this is one of the best loved resurrection narratives.[1] Leon Morris[2] describes it as a charming story, while Tom Wright says that "it is both a wonderful, unique, spellbinding tale, and also a model (and surely Luke knew this) for a great deal of what being a Christian, from that day to this, is all about."[3]

Two people walk away from their hopes. Caird and Wright both suggest that the two disciples are Cleopas and presumably his wife since they live in the same house. They suggest that if Cleopas is Clopas, then his wife is Mary who was one of the group of women at the cross (John 19:25). They have each other's company

1. In exploring this text I have consulted: Caird, *Gospel of Saint Luke*, 256–59; Carroll, *Luke*, 474–88; Edwards, *Gospel According to Luke*, 713–25; Green, *Gospel of Luke*, 840–51; Lieu, *Gospel of Luke*, 203–6; Marshall, *Gospel of Luke*, 889–903; Morris, *Luke*, 355–59; Nolland, *Luke 18:35—24:53*, 1194–1209; Talbert, *Reading Luke*, 226–33; Wilcock, *Message of Luke*, 205–11; Wright, *Luke for Everyone*, 291–98.

2. Morris, *Luke*, 355.

3. Wright, *Luke for Everyone*, 293.

but they feel rejected and alone. They expect no one to join them. They are not travelling far but walk as if they are carrying heavy burdens. Marshall and Nolland identify Emmaus as a village some three and a half miles west of Jerusalem called Amwas which, if so, the distance of seven miles would equate to the round-trip journey by the disciples.

From this passage we learn about the resurrection of Jesus. Jesus suddenly appears at the disciples' side on their journey and then suddenly disappears from their supper table. It is then that they realise the truth that he is not subject to the limitations of time and place, and that he is no longer dead, but alive. They thought him to be a flesh-and-blood stranger. In retrospect their failure could suggest a supernatural restraint until their minds were prepared for the staggering revelation, which came through the breaking of bread. Like modern sceptics they were convinced that miracles do not happen. Jesus was dead. They thought that he would be the messiah of Jewish nationalist expectation who would free Israel from Gentile domination, and that hope had proved illusory.

Carroll notes that there are several important motifs in this account: the disciples' misconception and lack of understanding; overcome by Jesus' interpreting of Scripture in the light of his passion, and interpreting the passion in the light of the scriptures; and the revelation-bearing hospitality at the meal table. This prepares for the continuing story in Acts.[4] He observes that there is circular structure of: travel from Jerusalem to Emmaus; eyes closed; eyes opened; travel from Emmaus to Jerusalem. Edwards and Green note the deficiency in Cleopas' interpretation of the passion, and it is Jesus who draws attention to their lack of understanding. Jesus notes their slowness to believe the scriptures, from which Carroll concludes that the Jerusalem they had left was bereft of Jesus and with the crucifixion it was bereft of hope.[5] Edwards notes the irony of this situation, where living disciples discuss the dead Jesus, while the living Jesus speaks with the lifeless disciples.[6]

4. Carroll, *Luke: A Commentary*, 474.
5. Carroll, *Luke: A Commentary*, 484.
6. Edwards, *Gospel According to Luke*, 716.

(a) The Encounter

From their conversation we learn that the women have discovered the empty tomb, resulting in a mixture of fear, joy, confusion and disbelief. Cleopas and his wife have left for home; behind them they have left those sad, tragic, and traumatic events. A seven-mile walk, if that is what it was, from Jerusalem to Emmaus would have taken at least two hours; and on this day their pace, no doubt, would have been much slower because of their emotional state. Their conversation is heavy with sorrow (v. 17) and disappointment (v. 21) and sheer bewilderment (vv. 22–24). As they walk, a stranger joins them, he may have caught up with them unnoticed; they were so engrossed in their own concerns they did not see the stranger coming. The stranger asks them what they are talking about, which seems to have made them so sad. Cleopas' reply is sharp, "Are you the only visitor in Jerusalem who doesn't know the things that have been happening there these last few days?" The stranger invites them to tell him: "What things? Tell me about it." So, Cleopas tells the story of Jesus.

Their story is made up of the ministry of Jesus in word and action, the crucifixion that completed it, and the hope of resurrection, which filled that ministry with meaning. We have the empty grave and the witness to that fact. We have everything here except a personal word from the living Christ, which would in turn bring the facts alive. He was even there with them, but still their hearts remained cold. There is no gospel without the experience of Jesus alive.

Nolland notes that these disciples have not responded to the witness of the scriptures, and that it is Easter faith that gives a particular focus to the reading of the Old Testament scriptures.[7] Jesus dispels their disillusionment through expounding the scriptures. The burden is within them. It is a spirit of sadness, disappointment and bewilderment, but above all there is disillusion. They did not expect what had happened. They were not prepared for this change of direction. Their hopes had been high. They had been

7. Nolland, *Luke*, 1208.

sustained by someone they had come to know and trust. But now it was over. He had left the scene and they felt marginalized by former companions who were having a different experience. They did not know it but it was all about to change.

So begins the story of the walk to Emmaus. It is written from the point of view of the two travellers. But there is another way of telling it. He joined their Sabbath walk. He matched his pace to theirs and listened to what they were saying. He was in no hurry to speak but simply took in what was going on. He knew them but he realised they had lost the ability to recognize him. So he began to dismantle their self-absorption by a question. It was not a threatening question. He invited himself into their conversation by asking an obvious question, and as a result everything changed.

One story looked at from two perspectives. From the first it is about lost hopes and the grief of disillusionment. From the other it is about the companionship of the risen Christ. More than that it can be said that the Emmaus Road story encompasses the reality of the people's experience of God through both Testaments. Scripture describes the pathways of God among his people. They were a people who are often walking in the wrong direction and not able to recognize the presence of God with them. The pathways of God were walked by priests and prophets, kings, and prostitutes who carried within a response to God that only came into full view in the grace and truth of Jesus.

Two disciples meet the risen Christ though they do not recognize him. They proceed to recount their disappointment at dashed hopes, and ironically tell Jesus his own story. Beginning with Moses and the prophets Jesus explains to them that the whole of Scripture pointed forward to himself. Then in the breaking of bread he is revealed to them. Hooker concludes that what is important in this story is the necessity for Jesus to suffer these things, and that he is revealed in the breaking of bread and in the scriptures. We can observe that what is more significant is that they do not need to be in Jerusalem or to observe the empty tomb to be in the presence of the Lord.[8]

8. Hooker, *Endings*, 54.

Luke 24 brings Luke's account of the Gospel to its end. Luke 24:1 and 24:52–53 frame Luke's account of the resurrection, and indicate that he is describing a beginning. Through the fact that we begin with 24:1, the first day of the week, we perceive that this is a new era, a new creation, a whole new world coming into being,[9] and conclude with Luke's version of the Great Commission for the mission of Christ into the future in the power of the Spirit (Luke 24:45–49).

The Emmaus Road shows a human touch, Luke's unfailing concern about the human condition—ordinary people and their needs met by the message of salvation in Jesus. The conversation of the two disciples is full of sorrow, disappointment, and lack of understanding. They are in need of help, and the stranger's question leads them to rehearse the facts about Jesus. In response to their observations, Jesus expounded the Old Testament Scriptures which speak of Christ. For us the Scriptures including the apostolic witness are a living testimony to the living Christ, his ministry and mission.

Wilcock observes that Jesus' words make sense of the seemingly meaningless jigsaw of events: "Were not our hearts burning within us while he talked to us on the road, and opened the Scriptures to us?" (Luke 24:32) Edwards quotes from Augustine and Anselm in describing this as "faith seeking understanding," but then observes that until the living Jesus is recognised Cleopas' knowledge will not lead to understanding.[10] There is a parallel here with the words of Simeon, moved by the Spirit to recognise the promised Messiah in the baby Jesus (Luke 2:28–32) and the prophetic words about his passion (Luke 2:34–35).

This is the nub of the problem for many folks we meet in life, and even among some who join in the worship of the church—we talk about the joy, peace, and the reality of the presence of Jesus in our lives, but there is no joy unless the gospel facts become alive in our own personal experience of the living Lord Jesus. We each need to invite Jesus to invade and share our lives. We are able to

9. Wilcock, *Message of Luke*, 206.

10. Edwards, *Gospel According to Luke*, 715.

affirm that life has meaning, and that that meaning is to be found in Christ. It is his words to us that do this, just as his words made sense of the jigsaw of pieces that the women saw at the tomb and of the story that Cleopas tells on the road to Emmaus.

Our testimony is of our own experience of Jesus accompanying us on the journey of faith. Each of us has a personal story to tell—a journey of faith; of ecstasy and pain; of loneliness and of the company of others; of doubts and of certainties. We must find ways of sharing these stories in our worship and fellowship together, and in the witness of our daily lives.

(b) The Meal and the Revelation

Two disciples returning from Jerusalem and journeying to Emmaus are discussing what has recently happened. They are joined by a stranger who encourages them to believe the Old Testament prophets that the Messiah must suffer before he is glorified. By this time they have reached their destination and invite their unknown companion to share hospitality overnight. While they are eating, he breaks the bread in a way that must have been familiar from previous occasions, and they realize that the stranger is Jesus. They realize too how his explanation of the Old Testament Scriptures has already filled their hearts with emotion, which is now shown to be justified.[11]

Marshall states that the objections to the historicity of this story are weak as the story fits with other traditional resurrection stories. The initial blindness of the disciples is more theological than fictional and has parallels with other resurrection appearance narratives. The account of the risen Lord looking different is in common with other accounts. During the journey, while these disciples are discussing the things that have taken place, Jesus draws near and walks beside them. The two disciples' failure to recognize and then their recognition of Jesus is presented in the words

11. Marshall, *Gospel of Luke*, 889.

"prevented" and "opened," which Edwards[12] observes are divine passives indicating a divine agency. They were therefore prevented from recognizing him, presumably by God. This dramatic concealment is more likely due to spiritual blindness on the part of the disciples than something unusual about Jesus' appearance. Its purpose, states Marshall, is to prepare the disciples for the revelation of the risen Jesus by a fresh understanding of the prophecies about the resurrection. It may also have the purpose of showing later followers that it is possible to be aware of the risen Jesus without being able to see him (as in Jesus' words in John 20:29).

The disciples assume that Jesus is also a pilgrim returning from the festival. Hence their question as to whether he alone is the only one who doesn't know what everyone else has been talking about in Jerusalem. Marshall observes that the mention of the third day (Luke 24:21) may indicate the Jewish belief that by the fourth day the soul has left the body, or it may possibly be a reference to the time since the crucifixion. In verse 26 the stranger states the basic pattern of events concerning the Messiah in a way which implies that the disciples should have been aware of it already. Whatever Jewish expectations may or may not have been, the stranger is clearly taking up the passion predictions made by Jesus (Luke 9:22, 44; 18:31–33). We then have a summary statement (v. 27) of a long discourse in which the stranger picks out the messianic passages from the Old Testament.

The stranger, when they reach Emmaus, gives the disciples the opportunity to invite him to stay. Nolland observes that the disciples press hospitality on the stranger (cf. Gen 18:3, 19:2, and Heb 13:2). But the meal scene for Carroll immediately inverts the roles of hospitality-providing host and guest. Jesus takes the bread and breaks it—Jesus the guest-become-host resumes his customary practice during his ministry.[13] The disciples' memories activated by Jesus' re-enactment of his meal practice leads to recognition. Once again Jesus appears at a meal, and Marshall comments that "it was because Jesus had appeared at meal times that the church

12. Edwards, *Gospel According to Luke*, 714.
13. Carroll, *Luke: A Commentary*, 486.

expected his presence at the Lord's Supper."[14] The action of taking and breaking the bread in verse 30 recalls Jesus' action at the Last Supper and serves to identify Jesus to the disciples. The effect of the revelation leads the disciples to reflect on how they had felt when Jesus opened the scriptures—the risen Jesus was already making himself known to them as he spoke to them. The suggestion may be made that this is a pointer for later believers to recognize their inward warmth of heart springing from the presence of the risen Lord. Marshall concludes that the report of the two disciples back in Jerusalem confirms the appearance to Peter (and vice versa we might say). Lieu[15] observes that these two disciples are now able to re-interpret their experience on the road or as she notes "on the way"—the Christian journey where Christians are "followers of the way" (Acts 9:2, 19:9, 23).

Two factors are confirmed: the conversation and interpretation of Scripture; and the breaking of bread. We can conclude with Marshall that "in the reading of Scripture and at the breaking of bread the risen Lord will continue to be present, though unseen."[16]

(c) How This Story Fits into the Biblical Context

In Luke's gospel story of the two travellers we have the Old Testament experience of God and his people squeezed into a journey of seven miles. In this journey away from Jerusalem they walk with the nameless thousands who populate the ancient books of the Jewish faith. Some we know such as: Abraham and Sarah, Jacob, Moses, Elijah, Naomi, Hannah, David, Solomon, Hosea, Jeremiah, Qoheleth, and many psalmists; all of whom had a similar experience. There is a record throughout the Old Testament of intermittent faith and trust. The two knew it all. They could retell the story of the ministry of Jesus the mighty prophet and the crucifixion that brought their hopes to a frightening end. It would seem that

---

14. Marshall, *Gospel of Luke*, 898.

15. Lieu, *Gospel of Luke*, 205.

16. Marshall, *Gospel of Luke*, 900.

not even news of the empty grave and the verification of witnesses could reenvision the two companions. They, like Old Testament believers, were trapped in their own way of seeing things. They had no frame of reference with which to reinterpret the hope they had placed in Christ. This resurrection story is a turning point in which we move on to a future where faith and trust become more certain. It is a future where Christ opens the scriptures, explores the necessity of his suffering, pours out his Spirit to warm cold hearts, is known in the breaking of bread, and keeps on calling a new people of God into being.

Caird maintained that what Luke is claiming is that, under-lying all the Old Testament writings, Jesus detected a common pattern of God's dealings with his people, which was meant to foreshadow his own ministry.[17] God's purpose in creation was the emergence of a holy people, dedicated to God's service, and in a world organized to resist his will, this purpose is only achieved as the people themselves are prepared to undergo humiliation and suffering. Some of this at the hands of others, some through their own sin and God's punishment, and some as vicarious suffering for others (as suggested in the Servant Songs of Isaiah). The common pattern is the Exodus pattern: the people brought by God from humiliation of Egyptian bondage to the glory of a new day, their salvation history celebrated through the Passover. Now Jesus atones for the sins of the nation and his followers find redemption celebrating their salvation story in the Eucharist.

Hooker maintains that Luke stands in the middle of time. He looks back to what God has done in the past and forward to what God will do in the future.[18] She observes that the start of Luke's account goes back to the Jewish context, with the quote from Hannah's prayer (Luke 1:46–53, cf. 1 Sam 2:1–9), with the prophetic words of Zechariah (Luke 1:67–80), Mary (Luke 1:46–55) and Simeon (Luke 2:29–32). It continues with the genealogy which goes back to Adam (Luke 3:23–38). Jesus will bring salvation to

---

17. Caird, *St. Luke*, 258.
18. Hooker, *Endings*, 50.

his people and also in promise to the Gentiles (Luke 2:32).[19] Luke makes plain by the use of the Old Testament that the story of Jesus is the continuation of what happened in the past, and his second volume makes clear that the story of the apostles is the continuation of the story of Jesus. Luke's two books are joined by the report of the women at the tomb, who see and hear the angels and "remember the words of Jesus"—probably his prediction about betrayal, death, and resurrection. They report to the disciples who do not at first accept what the women have witnessed, but the Emmaus Road passage and the commissioning of the disciples in Luke 24 leads us into the continuing mission of Christ.

In her conclusion, Hooker draws a comparison between the end of Luke's account of the Gospel and the end of the Book of Acts. In Acts 28:23, 30–31 Paul explains about Jesus from Moses and the Prophets just as the risen Jesus had done on the Emmaus Road. Paul is continuing both the teaching of Jesus and the mission that Jesus entrusted to the disciples, to proclaim the Gospel.[20]

(d) Reflections on Emmaus and the People We Meet

The Emmaus Road story provides a powerful key to how disillusionment can be turned around and become again for many a pathway of God toward the rewards of hope. For many people it is a long journey. It is a journey through experiences and places where God is close but hidden. It is a journey away from the constraints of other people's certainties. It is a journey away from ways of belief and faith which may be found wanting. It will offer resting places where Scripture will be reexamined through the eyes of Christ. It is a journey shaped by our unique story, that validates our story, and encourages us to see the possibility of a Christ-encounter within that story. It is a journey toward a new community of belief whose mission is defined by the grace and truth of God in

19. Hooker, *Endings*, 49.
20. Hooker, *Endings*, 59–62.

Jesus. This is the journey that the risen Christ shared with Cleopas and his companion in the space of a few hours.

We can build on the model Jesus presents to us on the road to Emmaus; Jesus models for us a way in which to understand people. To set Jesus' ministry, his words and stories, in context we might go back to the beginning, to the opening chapters of the Gospel according to Luke. At twelve years of age Jesus is taken to the Temple for the first time; from that time on we might suggest that he remains in "his Father's house" (cf. John 5:19–23 and 14:1–3) doing and obedient to his Father's will. For the first seventeen years of his adult life (13–30), from his *bar mitzvah*, when he became a son of the law, until his baptism by John, when he is publicly declared Son of God, he grows in spiritual as well as physical maturity; in wisdom and understanding of the law (Luke 2:42; 3:23). This is seventeen years of life among the ordinary people, sharing the common life of the village community of Nazareth, perhaps occasionally journeying to a family celebration in another village, for example a wedding celebration at Cana (John 2:1–11), or the annual pilgrimage to Jerusalem for the Passover or one of the other major Jewish religious festivals.

The picture is of village life; a small local synagogue, where Jesus would have learned the Torah; obedience to parents; work in the local building and furniture trade as a carpenter alongside his father. This was not a significant place to grow up, from a worldly point of view, as Nathaniel was quick to point out to Philip: "Can anything good come out of Nazareth?" (John 1:46) But for us this upbringing and life experience was extremely important. This was self-emptying (Phil 2:7); this was the place where Jesus learned about people and life in the raw; this is where Jesus entered into the people's stories. Jesus is obedient and committed to God's self-emptying, God's incarnation among ordinary human beings. This is where God shares my life, and shares my experiences, and understands what it means to be me. And at his baptism in the Jordan Jesus receives his Father's affirmation: "This is my beloved son with whom I am well pleased" (Luke 3:22).

Here is a model for our ministry and involvement in the mission of Christ. Understanding people, sharing their lives, drawing on our own experience of living the life that our friends and neighbors also live. We know our neighbors' lives and questions, their joys and concerns, because they are ours also. We understand the impact of the latest terrorist atrocity, or the latest pointless killing of a young person on our streets or the tensions in politics and economics, because we share the feelings of sorrow, anger, fear, anxiety, and despair. But we are also able to speak of how our faith in Christ, suffering with and for the world in love, has supported and strengthened us through all this, and given us peace. For this reason, it is often the congregation, who are the experts in the local mission of the church, rather than the pastor. They share the same life as their neighbors and are in the best position to be the church's evangelists.

So, as we think about all those people with whom we are in contact, we remind ourselves that for many of the people we will meet life does not make sense. For many people Jesus is a character in history (perhaps) or simply an expletive to express exasperation. We know lots of people who are asking questions, expressing their view that the world is a terrible or even terrifying place, or simply struggling through a life which has no hope (except a win on the lottery), and which is controlled by fate. How do we share the gospel with such people; how do we minister to them. Like Cleopas and his wife, with whom Jesus walked on the road to Emmaus, they may have some knowledge of the ministry, crucifixion and claims of an empty tomb, but this is not helping them. So, how do we help people to understand and to find the meaning to life that we have found in Jesus. The answer is that we must follow Jesus' pattern:

First, we listen to people; we invite them to tell us their story; to recount their experiences of life and the world; to tell us what they understand about those experiences; what they mean to them and for them.

Second, we share with them what we know of Jesus; how his story and God's story in the Bible makes sense; how his word to us has made sense of our lives; how we have experienced Christ in all areas and aspects of our life.

Third, then we stay with people whatever they think or believe; we are not put off; we demonstrate our care, interest and love; we eat with them. We are encouraged in this approach through the success of *Alpha*-type meetings.

Last, we seek to follow Jesus' example: he did not dominate the occasion, insisting that they agree with him and accept his interpretation. As he had done in his ministry bound to one place and time so he continued in his unfettered resurrection life—he left them with the experience and to seek the meaning. A meaning which needed the support and guidance of a community called together in his name. This was their experience when they returned to the group of disciples in Jerusalem (Luke 24:33–35), and the further confirmation, when Jesus reveals himself to them all (Luke 24:36–43).

I intend to use the Emmaus Road story as the central motif in this text. For the story is more than an event in time and space. It is an experience for any time and any space. It provides a pathway for anyone who wishes move from disillusion to hope. It is a journey of repentance, in the sense that it requires a change of mind and a willingness to let go what has lost its power to set hearts afire. Nolland notes that this account reflects the early Christian conviction that it was only through an encounter with the risen Lord that the key was given for understanding that the passion and resurrection–exaltation were already witnessed to by the Scriptures.

Marshall and Nolland note the literary quality of the Emmaus Road story, which has features in common with the story of the Ethiopian eunuch in Acts 8:26–40: the journey motif, ignorance of scripture, explanation of Jesus' suffering from scripture, a request for the interpreter to stay longer, the sacrament, in this case baptism, and the sudden disappearance of the interpreter.

Nolland observes Luke's purpose in identifying the life of Jesus mirrored in the life of the early church.[21] Luke wants to make the point that the Christians of his day were able to have the living Lord

21. Nolland, *Luke*, 1200.

made known to them in their "breaking of bread" in a manner that was at least analogous to the experience of the Emmaus disciples. It is clear that this is also a story to guarantee the resurrection: it is the fulfilment of the Old Testament; and witness to the risen Lord's appearance to his disciples, and their recognition of Jesus.[22]

We find this pattern repeated in Paul's teaching in the Book of Acts. Although approaching the good folk of Athens from an evangelistic/apologetic stance (Acts 17:16–34), Paul takes a similar approach to that of Jesus on the Emmaus Road. Paul went and joined in the debates and discussions taking place in the market place, where the thinkers and philosophers gathered. The Epicureans thought the gods to be distant and uninterested in human affairs and so they emphasised chance and pleasure, while the Stoics were fatalists and saw ease or pain as something to be endured. They were interested in any new ideas and were intrigued by Paul's account of two new gods: Jesus and Resurrection. They invited him to the more formal surroundings of the Areopagus—the council place, where trials and important issues were debated. We can observe that the Epicurean pleasure seekers and the Stoic doom and gloom mongers are alive and well and living in our communities. Paul says "I've been looking at all your temples, with all the statues to different gods. You even have a temple to 'An Unknown God'—just in case! Just in case there was one you didn't know about who would be angry not to receive your worship, your adoration and your gifts. Fantastic! I'm truly amazed!" "Let me tell you about your unknown god, who I know, and who I have met. He is the creator of the universe, he is the source of life, he guides the history of the planet, he is concerned for every human being, he wants each of us to enjoy the world he has made, and to have a loving relationship with each other and with God. He has done this through his Son and he has given the proof of this to everyone by raising him from the dead."

Paul's was a frontier situation but so is ours, and he gives us an example of the sort of conversation we might have with our culture. In early twenty-first century Britain the story of the gospel

22. Marshall, *Gospel of Luke*, 890.

is not well known outside the church. The language, practices, values, buildings and meetings of the church are alien to many people. Many churches have become communities cut off from society, and so there is a need to listen to others who we meet on "the road." There is a need for participation, interaction, dialogue, reflection, debate, argument and the support of others. We do this through such conversations.

(e) Supper and the Risen Christ

A key feature of the Emmaus Road story is the meal at which the risen Christ is revealed. There is a great deal of importance in telling each other the story which is celebrated through the Lord's Supper. We move away from individualism and "what I get out of church," to a recognition and understanding of the body of Christ. To make this clear, we want to bring together the celebration of the Lord's Supper and the Emmaus Road experience, which links conversation, relationships and communion.[23]

Cleopas and his wife are clearly intrigued by the stranger's conversation; by now they have reached Emmaus, and they offer hospitality. This is the Jewish way—feeding and housing the stranger. Jesus accepts their invitation, and joins them for supper in their home. The best way of getting to know people is around a meal table. Jesus sat down to eat with them; took bread and gave thanks for it; broke the bread and gave it to them; they recognized him; and he disappeared. When they reflected on how they felt; they realize the truth of the good news; no longer sad; they rush back to Jerusalem to tell the eleven disciples (we might wonder how much faster they covered the return journey).

In Jerusalem they find that Jesus is risen: he has appeared to Peter; and as they tell their story, Jesus appears to all of them. Returning to Jerusalem to tell their joyful good news, they find their experience confirmed by the experience of the community of faith. Our experiences of God, likewise, should be shared with

23. Weaver, "Spirituality", 135–67.

the community of faith. Testimony is an important part of our life together—we encourage each other. Also, our experiences need to be checked by the community of faith, for sometimes we may be mistaken. We might observe Paul's criteria for testing spiritual gifts and experiences: Is it in accordance with Scripture? Does it accord with love? Does it build up the church?

Eleanor Kreider aptly describes an "impulse toward commonality" which is expressed in the celebration of the Lord's Supper. She rightly asserts that joining together in worship is in stark contrast to the "primary impulse of Western individualism."[24] Kreider challenges the church to recognise that the way we take communion makes a difference, for we act out or perform our communion theology. A key question is whether we partake only as individuals or also as a community. "Dead ritual" is easy to spot, since a moribund rite is no substitute for reality; it can be seen, for example, in the breaking of bread and pouring of wine in a congregation of people whose lives are in no way broken for the world or poured out in love for their neighbors.[25] The language of ritual speaks most powerfully when it is deeply connected to the circumstances of people. In retelling the story of God's creating, redeeming and liberating love, we find that the Spirit is able to minister to our individual and community needs. Celebration of the Lord's Supper can be seen as both communicative and commemorative. First, the Supper communicates as a means of grace: that is, Christ is present, we are conjoined by the Spirit, and there is a renewal of our covenant with Christ and with each other. Donald Baillie helpfully asks if we are saved by faith or by the sacraments. His answer is: by neither, but by God, who saves us through faith and therefore partly by the sacraments that he uses to awaken and strengthen our faith.[26] Second, the Supper commemorates. There is remembrance and response to memory. We stand between memory and hope, between incarnation and consummation. Hope looks to the future, while memorial looks to the past, and we cry *Marana tha!*

24. Kreider, *Communion*, 242.
25. Kreider, *Communion*, 153.
26. Baillie, *Sacraments*, 101.

Come Lord Jesus, looking for a coming which is both present and eschatological.

Thus we are not celebrating with empty symbols, but ones which enable us to participate in the death and resurrection of Christ. We recognize this when we consider the Jewish understanding of the Passover, which in turn is reflected in the New Testament presentation of the Lord's Supper and of baptism (see 1 Cor 10; Rom 6:1–14; 1 Cor 6:12–20). To understand the connection, we need to think about the power of story. In the Passover story God leads the people to safety through the Reed Sea and makes a covenant with them at Mount Sinai. They go on remembering all of this at an annual celebration of being the people of God (Deut 16:1–4). It was this meal that Jesus celebrated with his disciples on that fateful Passover eve, where Jesus gives new meaning to the Passover—it is a new covenant of forgiveness and love, for friends and enemies, which is in Christ and his death. We are to become people of this new covenant through becoming one with Jesus in his death and resurrection. As the church takes up the celebration of this story self gets in the way and Paul rightly attacks the self-centredness of the Corinthian church. "It's not the Lord's Supper that you are celebrating, when you take the bread and wine during your meal. It can't be the Lord's Supper because you are divided—there's no love being shown here" (1 Cor 11:17–22). There is little evidence of the new commandment of love that Christ demonstrated and called for at the Last Supper (1 Cor 11:23–29). This meal is to be a celebration of being the people of God, the body of Christ, a loving fellowship. We are now part of this story.[27]

One problem arises when we place the story in a book, it removes it from the drama of the liturgy within the community. It also leads to individualism and debate, where everyone has their own private interpretation. The gospel is no longer focused in a person but in a book. In some ways the institutional church has lost the emphasis on a living faith, and we need to rediscover the journeying, pilgrim church, who tell, listen to, and live the ongoing

27. A fuller exploration of Passover and Lord's Supper is found in Weaver, *Outside-In*, 30–32.

story. The Passover or Lord's Supper help us to recover such story-telling, for the Supper is the place where the story is retold, reenacted, and where the people enter into the story. The community grows together as its members celebrate the Lord's Supper, recalling the story of the Jewish Passover and the story of Jesus' last meal with his disciples on the way to the cross. But then we recognize that each individual Christian's story is a part of this story as it reflects the activity of God in our lives. Out of the church's story comes the vision of the kingdom of God, what God wants to do and is able to do in lives that are open to his purposes. Given the reality of our sin, especially in terms of self-centredness, this vision of the kingdom is always "not yet," and this is a limiting factor in all our praxis. Yet American theologian and educationalist Thomas Groome is right to hold out the goal to us:

> In the community encounter between our own stories and the Story, between our own visions and the Vision, we can come to "know God" in an experiential/reflective manner. It will be a praxis way of knowing that arises from our own praxis, from the praxis of our community of pilgrims in time, and from the praxis of God in history.[28]

The New Testament scholar C.F.D. Moule is right to state that the gospel is more than declaration, something to read and know; it is experience, and faith is a lived faith. God's unique action in Christ is not some "dead and static thing," it is the living God at work through the church as the body of Christ. The incarnation is a unique point in history, but "if it is continuous with the People of God before it, then in some sense redemption must be continued with the Church after it."[29] This is what happens for Cleopas and his wife in their home in Emmaus on Easter evening, and is the promise of an encounter with the risen Christ that we can expect in the Eucharist.

28. Groome, *Education*, 193.
29. Moule, *Sacrifice*, 32–33.

(f) Some Pointers for Further Exploration

There are a number of aspects to the Emmaus Road story and each needs attention:

- Life experience—taking it seriously
- The often disillusioning impact of daily life
- The companionship of Christ—learning how to affirm it
- Telling our story in the presence of the Risen Christ—learning how to share it
- Allowing Scripture to speak to our story
- Enabling transformation—invitation, meal, revelation
- Moving into the experience of hope restored
- Witness to others[30]

The rest of this book will explore these themes.

Fiddes reminds us that communities are formed by the stories they tell:

> Remembering the story allows us to encounter the same God who is present in the community in the past, in exodus, crucifixion, and resurrection. In telling the story we encounter the crucified and risen Lord anew, and this forms the community as the representative of this Lord in the world.[31]

The gospel story includes resurrection life and power (Eph 1:20); the good news of Jesus crucified and risen, and present by his Spirit, transforms life today. The gospel is not the gospel if we do not experience resurrection life now (John 11:25–26). We can share the stories of being the church in the power of the resurrection.

This is the gospel we profess, and which we are called to share. The proof is ultimately seen in the post-Easter changed lives of the disciples of Jesus, and continues to be seen in transformed

30. I am indebted to David Kerrigan (the former General Director of BMS World Mission) for these observations.

31. Fiddes, *Tracks*, 169.

lives of those who trust Jesus with their lives. Like the man that I spoke with at an *Agnostics Anonymous* group (referred to as "Lions thrown to the Christians") at Spring Harvest, Easter time some years ago. He had drifted away from church and saw no way back. I suggested to him that he read the parable of the prodigal son in the Good News version of the Bible. He went off to buy a copy. He came back to see us the next day—you could see the transformation—glowing, no longer dull and downcast. This is an encounter with the risen Christ: "I am the resurrection and the life" (John 11:25), "I have come that they might have life, and have it to the full" (John 10:10). It had been an Emmaus Road experience for that man.

2

My Emmaus Journey and Beyond

IN MY LIFE THUS far there have been special experiences which have been helpful to my understanding of and growth in faith. Some of these may be described as "thin places." It is therefore helpful to begin with the nature of "thin places" as expressed by the Celtic saints and others in church history; how we understand "thin places" theologically and how we might encourage others to reflect theologically on such experiences. They are those places, events, maybe even people, in whose company we experience the presence of God in an especially real way. Whatever the circumstance, which can be as unique as one person is to another, one thing is common: a "thin place" is a location or moment in which our sense of the divine or sacred is more pronounced, where the space between the transcendent and the commonplace is exceptionally narrow.

"Thin place" is a description that has been used for over fifteen hundred years. It is a term that comes from the mystical world of Celtic spirituality and the Celtic Christians, who were deeply connected to the natural world and considered every aspect of life to be filled with the presence of the divine, even in the ordinary, when we are open to being aware of God in the everyday experience of living. While historically the ancient Celts viewed thin places as locations or moments in the cycle of the year where the veil between the world and the spiritual realm diminished and they could encounter those who had gone before them, today thin places are more commonly considered locations in which there is an undeniable connection to the sacred. Such places are the destination of pilgrimage, although many would find that the pilgrimage itself was a "thin place" where God seemed especially close.

There have been a variety of spaces and places which I have experienced that I would describe as "thin places." I would certainly want to recount my experience in the rose garden at the University of Central America, San Salvador, where the six Jesuit priests and their two housekeepers were tortured and murdered. But then, it is also relevant to consider the ways in which God has encountered me in the more "ordinary" places, which each of us might also experience. This can include God's word and presence in worship—I could speak of such an encounter at Spring Harvest in the 1980s. Then there are those special people whose presence brings God and the gospel into sharp focus—I could speak of conversations and walks with the Mennonite missionary to the UK, the late Alan Kreider or the leader of the Irish Baptist Network, Stephen Adams. There are places, for me in the countryside or along the sea shore, where the creator and creation explode in wonder and awe.

The Bible records what we, as third party observers, might describe as "thin places" for example: Jacob's ladder to heaven (Gen 28:10–17); Moses vision of a burning bush (Exod 3:1–6); Isaiah's vision of God in worship (Isa 6); Saul's encounter on the road to Damascus (Acts 9); Peter's rooftop invitation to a meal (Acts 10); and John's vision on Patmos (Rev 1:9–10). The following are some of my "thin places."

(a) Growing Up as a Scientist and a Christian

I was born in Cardiff, immediately after the Second World War, into a committed Baptist family. Growing up in a loving Christian home it became natural for me to have God in the equation of my thinking about the world in which I lived. Christianity was the air I breathed, with both my mother and my father committed to roles in the church and expressing their own faith through their daily lives. But growing up was more than church.

My father taught biology and at an early age he introduced me to many exciting aspects of the biological sciences. He named the plants and animals that I encountered in the garden or in the countryside, and I learned their correct Latin names, genera and species, and something of the classification of the plant and animal kingdoms. In our pond we had frogs and I enjoyed the spring time when we watched frogspawn develop through the various stages of tadpole to adult frog. I learned about caterpillars becoming chrysalids and then moths or butterflies. My father had a microscope at home and he showed me that the hairs on my head had a particular structure and that tap water was teeming with microscopic life—which, I can assure you, did not encourage me to drink it!—in fact, I made a conscious decision to stick to lemonade. Unconsciously, the scientist in me was being shaped through observation, questions, and provisional conclusions. Scientific questioning continued with chemical experiments in my junior years: growing copper sulphate crystals and halite crystals. But all this experimentation was brought to an abrupt end with experiments with rocket fuel when I was about twelve years of age—the powerful explosion followed by the shattering of glass and wood as our neighbour's window was wrecked by my rocket. My father confiscated the chemicals, but at least my mother forgave me. I learned a great deal about unqualified love and forgiveness at my mother's knee.

In 1961 two revolutions took place in my thinking and questioning. In the Spring of 1961 the School Scientific Society presented a Geology lecture: rocks, minerals and fossils, and the speaker ended his talk by showing us "potato stones" from the Triassic rocks of Penarth, on the coast near Cardiff. These were concretions, about the size of a large potato, which were filled with crystals. He offered to break one open and invited someone to come and see. I volunteered; as he broke it open he said, "You are the first person to see inside this nodule, since the moment it was formed, in fact, ever!" This was a "thin place" for me as I felt my connection with the creator. From that moment I was hooked; geology was to dominate my interest through school, university, and my first employment as a lecturer in geology.

In the Autumn of 1961 a second revolution took place in my life, when I made a personal profession of faith in Christ. The warm loving faith of Christian parents, especially the witness to God's grace that I daily saw in my mother, was something that then became my own personal experience. Looking back, I recognise that this was so much down to the grace of God and little to do with my own depth of understanding or commitment. It would be another ten years before I opened up the whole of my life to Jesus as both Savior and Lord.

For seventeen years these two strands of my life, Geology and Christian faith, would run in parallel, only occasionally intersecting. Throughout this period of my life, like a number of early scientists, I lived with "the book of God in one hand and the book of Nature in the other." As with Geology, so too for theology we are limited by space and time. Geological history lies millions and billions of years in the past and most rocks are buried deep below our feet. Likewise, there are no certain proofs of doctrinal statements made by the church, the transcendent God is beyond the universe of our experience, and the Christian faith is anchored in events some two thousand years ago. We rely on our faith and our personal experience of God with us day by day.

(b) Called to Preach and Called to Train

I was sitting in Belper Baptist Church, Derbyshire listening to the sermon, when I became aware that I was thinking about something other than the preacher's message. This I realise as a preacher is a common experience for congregations, especially when the sermon is boring or above their heads. But this was never my experience of the preaching ministry of the late Peter Grange.

I had, almost as if written on an autocue, a whole service, hymns, prayers, readings, and sermon. This was a vivid experience and was the turning point in my understanding of God's call on my life.

Having written down what I had "seen" and "heard," and having wrestled with its meaning, I went to see Peter Grange and told him of my experience. I asked him if this was a message from God that I should preach. He wisely answered that if God wanted me to preach it, a church would invite me to take their service. A few weeks later Sheila and I were in South Wales visiting our parents, and attended the church in Rhymney, where we had been married. They knew little of our Christian journey, but the church secretary asked me if I would like to preach at the church next time we were visiting. Shocked and surprised by this apparent immediate answer to prayer I agreed to preach a month or so later. I followed the service that had been "revealed" to me: prayers, hymns, readings, and sermon. At the end of the service almost every one of the 25 people present came up to me and commented on the helpful nature of the service and of hearing God's word for their own lives. The church secretary asked me how long I had been preaching, and I owned up to this being the very first time. He and others, after hearing my story, suggested that God was calling me to preach.

(c) Experiences of God's Grace in Ministry

In 1986 I experienced pastorally caring for three people who had cancer.

Jean and Gordon first came to the church in 1984, the year after Jean had undergone surgery for breast cancer. They were both in their mid-fifties. Married later in life, they had a daughter Julia, who was sixteen years old. They were committed Christians, and Julia was baptised a year after they joined the congregation. As members of a Particular Baptist Church, they were reformed in their theology, and believed that spiritual gifts had been restricted to the apostolic era. They were not happy about the church's freer style of worship, nor with those who urged the church along the path of spiritual renewal, but they persisted in their attendance "because of the biblically-based preaching and the teaching." It therefore came as a surprise when, one evening in 1986 as pastor I received the following phone call, from Jean: "John, I don't know if you have heard about my most recent visit to the doctor. I've been suffering with chest pains for the last few months, and my doctor sent me to the hospital for some tests. I went to see the consultant earlier this week and he has diagnosed an extensive tumour in the pulmonary membrane." Jean said that she had been reading the Scriptures and in James 5:14–15 it says: "Is anyone among you ill? Let them call the elders of the church to pray over them and anoint them with oil in the name of the Lord. And the prayer offered in faith will make them well; the Lord will raise them up." "John, you know what Gordon and I have always said about healing in the present day, but I would like you to follow this Scripture for me. I have asked the Lord that I might see Julia settled into adult life." After praying about this request with my fellow leaders we became convinced that God did want to heal Jean. We went to Jean's home and anointed her with oil and prayed that God would heal her of her cancer. We felt a deep assurance that God was answering our prayer. This took place on a Tuesday evening and Jean was due to go back to her consultant on the Wednesday for him to decide on a course of treatment. On Wednesday evening Jean phoned to tell us that the consultant was totally perplexed, the x-ray was clear, the cancer had completely disappeared. At church on Sunday, Jean shared her testimony in such a quiet and sincere way that the congregation accepted the news with a quiet and deep sense of thanksgiving, but with little "over-the-top" (Jean and Gordon's words) exuberance.

Bert had just received the news, his cancer was inoperable and he had less than two years to live. He contacted me, asking me to come round and pray for him. Bert was a lapsed church member, and now he was frightened and despairing. Over the months of talking and praying with Bert, his faith was renewed and he once again began to trust God for his life. Bert had recovered his relationship with God, and far from praying for or with Bert, he shared his prayers with me. The transformation was complete, when near the end of his life he told me: "When I wake up in the morning I thank God that he has brought me through the night, to a new day; and at the end of each day I commit my life into God's hands, knowing that whether I live or die, I am safe in God's hands." This was complete healing, and Bert had found true peace.

At the same time my mother was dying of liver cancer—a secondary cancer to bowel cancer, which had been successfully operated on five years earlier. I visited my mother in South Wales every week (a three hundred mile round trip from our home) and was privileged to share her faith through the experience of this illness. The Macmillan nurses were excellent, but they were really touched by my mother's faith and her real concern for their "minor" troubles rather than her own health. Her faith and peace as God accompanied her through her last months was a powerful witness to God's love.

Three people and three different stories of healing, which both strengthened me in my own faith and in my ministry to others.

(d) In Brazil—a Further Revelation of God in Nature

During a two month sabbatical study time with BMS World Mission, I was taken to see Foz do Iguaçu, in the Brazilian state of Paraná. It is one of the world's largest waterfalls with a length of some 2.7 kilometers. It straddles the border with Argentina, comprises hundreds of cascades, including the eighty-meter-high "Devil's Throat" at the heart of the complex, which can only be accessed from the Argentinian side. It is possible to walk, on an iron walkway into the very center of the falls, looking into the "Devil's Throat." The whole structure of the walkway trembles continuously, the sound of the river crashing over the falls and onto the rocks below is deafening—it is the most amazing sight of the power and wonder of nature that I have ever experienced. Over the falls there is a constant rainbow (or to be more accurate, series of rainbows), which drew my Christian heart back to the promises of the creator God (Gen 9:11–17). Here we find the first of God's covenants—a covenant with the whole of creation. But more than this, above the falls, where the river runs gently toward the falls there is a sign in Portuguese, a quote from the Psalms: "Mightier than the thunder of the great waters, mightier than the breakers of the sea—the Lord on high is mighty" (Ps 93:4). Once again I stood with the book of God's works in one hand and the book of God's word in the other—a revelation of God that brought my earlier geological career and my pastoral ministry together.

(e) In Nicaragua—the Joy of Worship and Fellowship

During another two month sabbatical with BMS World Mission I was privileged to visit missionaries and base communities in Nicaragua and El Salvador. In Nicaragua I visited the base community of Centro Cultural Heroes Y Mártires de Batahola for an evening service on a Sunday and an exploration of the base community in action on the Monday following. The base community, which has extensive space and various rooms is used on weekdays as a medical center with nurse and doctor, adult education of various sorts including English language, computing, sewing, art, and cooking. A tribute to the artistic gifts of those who attend the center are the murals of local life in bright primary colors that adorn all the walls. There is no charge for the teaching that is offered except that those who receive training are expected to go out to other communities to teach and train others in what they have learned.

The Sunday evening service is the weekly Mass. The two Presbyterian missionaries, with whom I was staying, and I were welcomed by Sister Margarita who explains that the Mass is ecumenical and all are invited to join and share. We were welcomed by the Priest and clapped by the congregation of over two hundred. The church had an orchestra of guitars and recorders, at least fifty strong, who accompanied the singing, which sounded beautiful and powerful and included parts of the Misa Campesina.[1] The sermon, delivered by the priest, Father Angel Torrellas, was as refreshing as the worship with Father Angel in continuous dialogue with the congregation—excellent communication which involved

1. "Misa Campesina."

the congregation all the time, an example I occasionally follow. Sharing wafers and wine with people from Costa Rica, Nicaragua, USA, Canada, Ireland and the UK to the sound of singing and the accompaniment of the orchestra left me thinking "if heaven is like this—Come Lord Jesus."

Yet it is a sad fact that this base community is established on a piece of land where two hundred and four young people were murdered by the troops of President Somoza just before the revolution victory of 1979. Now it is a place where young people are taught, find value, and go out to improve the lives of the community. The base community began with sewing classes and Father Angel led music classes. There were seventy-five women in the first sewing class. Sister Margarita began to discuss their lives in terms of faith and the Bible. By 1983 the Contra war was inflicting great destruction and the community of Batahola were burying young boys every week. There were shortages of almost everything and the center was distributing food. The Sunday Eucharist was central throughout this time. The church leaders lived with the people, listened to their concerns and responded to their needs, all of which was focused around the Eucharist. They sought to discover the meaning of life with the people, and the center grew based on all sorts of economic need. The various classes enabled the people to develop skills for working and to sell the products of their trades. Every year the people ask for new opportunities for work and learning, but all is focused in building God's Kingdom of justice, love and sharing.

(f) In El Salvador—Am I Ready to Lay Down My Life for God?

During my time in El Salvador I was invited to visit the Jesuit University of Central America in San Salvador. On entering the University I was offered the opportunity to visit the rose garden where on the morning of November 16, 1989, an elite battalion of the Salvadoran Army entered the grounds of the university with orders to kill Father Ignacio Ellacuría, who was an outspoken critic of the Salvadoran military dictatorship. They were to leave no witnesses. When it was all over, the soldiers had killed six Jesuit priests, a housekeeper and her daughter in cold blood. The Jesuits' Massacre is one of most notorious crimes of El Salvador's twelve-year civil war, which left over seventy-five thousand people dead. I was told that before entering the rose garden I was to look through a photograph album, which contained photographs of the bodies of those who had been tortured and murdered, so that I would understand the pain that the members of the university community felt. This was not a pleasant experience and I wondered what it is that enables one human being to brutalize and mutilate another? It is difficult to speak after such a visit. I signed the record of remembrance and then silently went to stand in the rose garden in front of a simple plaque of remembrance for those who had been killed. This was a deeply disturbing spiritual experience, yet at the same time the privilege of being encountered by God. I heard that clear voice speaking to me: "would you be prepared to do this for me? Lay down your life for truth and justice?" The silence was palpable and on a very hot lunchtime I felt cold shivers running through me. I knew the answer that I would wish to make, but I am not convinced that it could be easily made.

From here I was taken to the Cancer Hospital Chapel on the fifteenth anniversary of the assassination of Óscar Romero, Archbishop of San Salvador. He was shot and fell dead across the altar as he celebrated the Eucharist on 24 March 1980. It was said that he put himself in the place of others, putting them and their safety before his own. So many people gathered that afternoon from many countries and of many denominations, and protestant pastors served the Eucharist alongside the Catholic priests. I met nuns from Porthcawl, South Wales, and from Warren Point, in Northern Ireland, both places that I know well. It was a privilege to be a part of this celebration, but the question again rose in my thoughts: "would you be prepared to do this for me?" We share the peace together and we share the commission together to serve Christ in and for the world. Here I sense true solidarity—receiving bread and wine at the place where Romero died in his solidarity with the people for whom Christ died.

Through these experiences in El Salvador I reflected on the story of the German Count Nikolaus von Zinzendorf (1700–60)[2] who founded the Herrnhuter Brüdergemeine (a group of the Moravian Bretheren). At the age of eighteen years the Count had a profound spiritual experience. He stood in the Dusseldorf art gallery, gazing at a picture of Christ, crowned with thorns, blood trickling down his face. He was looking at Domenico Feti's painting *Ecce Homo* (Behold the Man). Underneath was the Latin inscription: "This I have suffered for you, but what have you done for me?" Chastened, Zinzendorf prayed that the Savior would draw him into the "fellowship of his suffering." Little did he know how fully that prayer would be answered. His evangelical passion was not always accepted and the Lutheran Church sought to exclude him. He propagated his ideas through the Moravian Episcopal Church and was a caring leader. His emphasis on the place of feeling in religion infused new life into Protestant orthodoxy.[3]

At the end of my time in El Salvador we went to a well-known view point, Pueto del Diablo (The Devil's Door)—fantastic cliffs and views. I was able to take some superb photographs but unfortunately I no longer have the photographs, or the camera, or my watch, nor my wedding ring, nor my money. We climbed to the top of one of the cliffs—quite a climb in the afternoon sun and enjoyed the view for a while. Then two young men approached with knives and we were robbed. But thankfully they left us unharmed. The next day before leaving for the airport I went to El Cordero de Dios (Lamb of God Church) for 8:00 am breakfast and farewell with the church members. A final song and prayer with really lovely people full of life, laughter and love. Its hard to imagine that within the previous five years a number of this congregation had been tortured, raped and imprisoned by government forces. The stories behind the present joy are of intimidation, false accusations, death threats, torture, prison. Many have seen loved ones disappear—presumed dead. Despite the peace treaty some live with the

---

2. "Nikolaus Ludwig," *Encyclopaedia Britannica.*

3. Cross and Livingstone, *Dictionary*, 512.

threat of the knock on the door and being faced by a death squad or simply former soldiers looking to rob.

It was hard to imagine all this sitting in a cool air-conditioned airport lounge awaiting my flight to Houston and then onward to London. "This I have suffered for you, but what have you done for me?"

(f) God's Love Revealed

There are some very praise-filled experiences which stick in our minds. While in Nepal with BMS World Mission, I visited Pokhara in the foothills of the Himalayas, but I was informed that it was the wrong time of year to see the mountains in their full splendour as they would be shrouded in clouds of the Monsoon season. In my journal I wrote the following for 28th January 2008:

> Awoke at 6.45am and looked out of my bedroom window, to my surprize the mountains of the Annapurna range were cloud free with the sun reflected in the snow covering the peaks. Quickly I pulled on some clothes and went up onto the roof of the apartment to look at the mountains—it was a truly breathtaking sight. I sang to myself *"Then sings my soul, my Saviour God to Thee, how great Thou art."* The triangular peak of the mountain that overlooks Pokhara is called Machapuchare, which means "fish tail." I am sitting on the roof watching the changing views of the mountains as the sun rises higher. As time passes the clouds descend and cover the mountains and the awesome sight is obscured. As I contemplated the view and while the peaks were still in sight, I read my Bible notes for the day, which began with the words of Henry Burton's hymn: *"There's a light upon the mountains, and the day is in the spring, when our eyes shall see the beauty and the glory of the King . . ."* Amen, my heart and mind cried out.

Once again in my life, God graciously affirmed his presence and love.

3

Reflections on My Journey

EMMAUS EXPERIENCES OR "THIN places" are part of a whole life lived in the presence of God. While these experiences are "high points" of our Christian experience to be treasured, they do allow us to reflect on the whole of our lives through the lens of God's ever present love and companionship. The story of the transfiguration in Luke 9 reveals the dangers that may be present in the most precious of our experiences—we want to hold onto them, we build "tabernacles" to preserve them only to find that our faith fails us when tested, just as Peter, James, and John's did when they descended from the mount of transfiguration.

Special times of being encountered by God are very important to us; special days and special services or anniversaries are important in our Christian life, but we must not try to preserve them; or simply long to repeat them. We have to live with the daily reality of our lives. This is our journey of faith; this is our daily worship of God. We come together on Sunday as the gathered church to encourage and equip each other for being the scattered church, during the rest of the week. We remember the special times and draw strength from them, just as Peter did, when reflecting upon his experience of the transfiguration (2 Pet 1:16–19a). Peter says, this is what it was like for me on the mountain with Jesus, Moses and Elijah, and this is how I now live in its light.

We move on to live for Jesus, to serve him in the world, through the power of the Holy Spirit, always remembering that the God who has encountered us in the past and today, on the Emmaus Road or in our "thin places," goes ahead of us and is with us until the end of time. The experiences are one part of my and your life story.

When Martin McGuinness died on 21 March 2017 various people commented both positively and negatively about his life as a terrorist turned peacemaker and politician. I was particularly impressed by the words of Ian Paisley jnr, the DUP MP for North Antrim, who said he took a Christian view when assessing McGuinness' legacy. His was that the Christian view of life does recognise that the beginning of a person's journey is important, "but it is how it finishes which is actually more important." He went on to say that "the journey of Martin McGuinness' life ended in a very different way to what people would have supposed it would have done." He was once a man who struck fear into people's hearts in Northern Ireland. "Yet he became the necessary man in government to deliver a stable and necessary peace, and that's a complex and remarkable journey," he added.[1]

Some thirty years ago I read the words of Bishop Stephen Neill who stated that Christians need to go through three conversions: a conversion to Christ, a conversion to his church, and a conversion to the world, for which Christ died.[2] These words certainly reflect the early part of my own journey of discipleship. We might describe these "conversions" as necessary stages in becoming "Kingdom people"—we in Christ and he in us.

As I reflect on my Christian journey of faith over the last sixty years, I am sadly concerned to see, through my preaching and teaching ministry, the common (although thankfully not universal) picture of a modern individualistic and consumerist church that has largely "lost the plot"—lost the vision of the community

1. Ian Paisley, "Tributes."
2. Address to the World Council of Churches, Evanston, Canada, 1954.

Jesus invited us to join. We are Christians assured of our personal salvation in Christ, believing that the Bible is the word of God, worshipping in churches that have good preaching, and which provide the right programmes for us and our children. This is fine up to a point, but I believe that my own faith story challenges such a safe, comfortable, and essentially selfish model of church, and perhaps, more importantly, provides a different perspective of a secure hope when faced with doubts and sorrows.

(a) Conversion to Christ

Some people that I know have experienced a "Damascus Road" conversion; a dramatic encounter with the truth of the gospel and a meeting with the risen Saviour in the midst of life. I have had the privilege, as a minister, of being with a number of people when they have experienced such a conversion as they have entrusted their lives to Christ. My own conversion has been the common experience of many others in the churches of which I have been a part. As part of a church going family, I attended weekly worship in our local Baptist church on a Sunday morning and was taught the Bible stories in Sunday School on Sunday afternoons. My parents were both involved in the life and ministry of the church, my father as a deacon and adult Bible Study leader, and my mother in leadership with the midweek women's meeting. Church was part of growing up and the faith of my parents and many others in the church fellowship was demonstrated in the ways in which they lived and treated others, inside and outside of the church. In my mind it was a natural progression to believe the things I saw and was taught and consider making the faith of my parents my own personal faith. I made a personal profession of faith and was baptised at the age of fifteen years, but it would be a further ten years before the full impact of this faith would invade all aspects of my life. This is all of the grace of God at work, it would be a further fifteen years before I discovered the term "prevenient grace" and its meaning—but this was my experience.

In 1971 I was appointed Lecturer in Structural Geology at what is now the University of Derby. We settled in Belper and on our first Sunday went to Belper Baptist Church. I'd grown up in a fairly typical Welsh non-conformist church, where any challenge to living out my faith beyond the church building seemed to have passed me by. I read my Bible sometimes, and I prayed occasionally, especially around exam times as I seem to remember! Beyond that, I would probably best be described as a "Sunday Christian." Again, the grace of God was at work in my story. When my wife and I moved to Belper my mother, being concerned for our Christian grounding in a local church, got hold of a Baptist Union Handbook and looked at the Derbyshire churches. She suggested we go to one of the largest of those churches, Broadway Baptist Church, Derby. However, on that first Sunday we got up late, and having no time to get to Derby, we went to the local church, where we found a warmth of welcome we had rarely experienced before. Belper Baptist Church had just called a young minister called Peter Grange. Peter's preaching was direct and clear and challenged my faith and life.

My understanding of the spiritual journey went through a conceptual revolution, as I recognized that the Christian faith was to be lived out in seven-day-a-week discipleship and not only when the church met together. After many years of singing George Herbert's hymn, "King of glory, King of peace," I finally heard the words:

> King of glory, King of peace, I will love thee;
> and that love may never cease, I will move thee . . .
> *Seven whole days, not one in seven,* I will praise thee;
> in my heart, though not in heaven, I can raise thee.
> Small it is, in this poor sort to enroll thee:
> e'en eternity's too short to extol thee.

I came to recognize that my faith and my teaching and research in geology were part of a whole; together they were what I was. I needed to avoid the dualism of a "Sunday faith" and a "secular occupation." I realized that it was through my life outside church that I gave witness to my faith. As a street pastor said to me many years later: "Just remember that you are the only Bible that most folk will ever read."

As I began to take 24/7 Christian discipleship seriously, I decided to give attention to the understanding of my studies in geology. As a child I had seen a demonstration of the complementarity of science and faith in the life of my biologist father, and I had already, as a student, explored the creation stories in Genesis. I knew that some people took the words of the biblical account of creation literally, but as someone immersed every day of the week in the discoveries, insights and implications of geological research this was not an option open to me.

As I looked at the text of Genesis 1–11 and read some general Bible commentaries I began to discover biblical criticism and to explore the meaning of the Genesis text. If all that I taught in my geology lectures was true then a literal interpretation of Genesis 1–11 was not possible. My engagement in the dialogue between Christianity and science began at this time. Science and faith in dialogue was not only important for my own faith and understanding of the ways in which God works in the world, but also was an important aspect of my witness as a Christian, especially with students and those who were not Christians.[3]

(b) Conversion to the Church as the Body of Christ

It was at Belper Baptist Church that I began to take seriously the fact that discipleship involved a commitment to the life of the local church. I became church secretary and a deacon at the ripe old age of twenty-five. Belper Baptist was a unique church in lots of ways and encouraging younger adults into leadership was one of them. The minister was twenty-four years old and the secretary twenty-five—probably a first in late twentieth century Baptist church life. The church adopted a Romans 12:3–8 model:

---

3. My exploration of the dialogue between science and Christianity is found in Weaver, *Christianity and Science*.

> For by the grace given me I say to every one of you: Do not think of yourself more highly than you ought, but rather think of yourself with sober judgment, in accordance with the faith God has distributed to each of you. 4 For just as each of us has one body with many members, and these members do not all have the same function, 5 so in Christ we, though many, form one body, and each member belongs to all the others. 6 We have different gifts, according to the grace given to each of us. If your gift is prophesying, then prophesy in accordance with your faith; 7 if it is serving, then serve; if it is teaching, then teach; 8 if it is to encourage, then give encouragement; if it is giving, then give generously; if it is to lead, do it diligently; if it is to show mercy, do it cheerfully.

This is something that I have sought to encourage throughout my ministry as a pastor and as a teacher. Recognising gifts, enabling and empowering others, delegating—letting others develop their gifts—a risky part of ministry. But this was a risk that others took in encouraging me in my calling. The risk of the mistakes that others may make; or worse still the risk that they may make a better job of it than me.

As time went on, I began to have a growing sense of God's call on my life and eventually came to the conclusion that if I was to give more time to ministry I would no longer be able to continue as a lecturer in Geology. Exploring the possibilities for further Christian ministry, Sheila and I considered opening a Christian bookshop, but realised that we had no experience for such an enterprise. But then God broke into my thinking in a dramatic way, the God-inspired gift of a complete service, as I have described earlier. I had always told other churches that I did not preach—I might be able to lecture to classes of one hundred or more students, but preaching was a completely different activity.

I now began to take seriously the possibility that God was calling me into pastoral ministry, and so I discussed all this with Peter Grange. One of his first questions was: What does Sheila think? I had to admit that I had not discussed this with my wife, because I realized the upheaval that would take place in our comfortable life of family, home, job and community. Wisely, he told me to talk with her and then for both of us to come back for conversation with him. I broached the subject with Sheila when Peter had left and much to my surprise, and indeed to her surprise, she was thrilled and thought that this was the right way forward in our Christian walk. We then realized that God was preparing both of us to hear his call.

This set in motion the process of discernment by others: the diaconate and Church Meeting of Belper Baptist Church, the Association Council, and a college selection conference. These were interesting experiences with some trepidation, some humour, and a great deal of affirmation. The church meeting asked us how we would cope with living in a "goldfish bowl." Our answer was simple: "Folk need to take us as we are; and we've never had nets or blinds on our windows." I believe that that same attitude marked my approach to pastoral ministry—I am the same person to whomsoever I am speaking and "what you see is what you get." The area superintendent suggested to the association council that they didn't have to worry about my call because I was giving up a senior lecturer's post. He then added that they didn't need to hear me read the Bible as I was a lecturer. As one who for many of the years following was involved in assessing the call of others, I am horrified at this initial part of my interview. It was of little help to me and so I challenged them to consider my call carefully as I very much wanted to be certain that in this step of faith I was following God's call. I was giving up security of employment and uprooting my family for an uncertain future. I was pleased that the ensuing questions were searching, and they agreed to commend me to the Baptist colleges. Sheila and I went to visit both Spurgeon's College, London and Regent's Park College, Oxford. Both interviews were most helpful and encouraging, although the different teaching methods were the factors that guided our decision. At Spurgeon's with larger student numbers the teaching was delivered mainly through lecture—I would in effect be moving from one side of the lectern to the other, whereas at Regent's the way of learning was through reading and essay writing, which was much closer to my role as a researcher in Geology. However, I was immensely encouraged by Ray Brown, the principal of Spurgeon's College who continued his interest in my progress over the next ten years.

Regent's Park College accepted me, they provided us with one of their new family apartments on the college site, and we began three years of academic and pastoral training. The tutors and fellow students at Regent's were very supportive and life-long friendships were formed. There was a good social life, including activities for the growing number of college children. Sheila quickly made a new circle of friends both inside and outside the college, especially with the teachers and parents at St Barnabas First School in Jericho. I was appointed as a student pastor at Drayton Baptist Church near Abingdon, a role that I followed for almost all three of my years in College. A small loving fellowship, where I learned so much about pastoral ministry: my first wedding, baptism, funeral, infant thanksgiving—we laughed and cried together and they graciously put up with my mistakes and failings as a minister in training.

I experienced much encouragement and affirmation while at Regent's, but one encounter with God stands out above all others during my college life. It was during my first term exploring the Old Testament with all the teasing questions about historical accuracy and authorship, while also settling in as a family, missing friends and the home we had made in Belper. I was going through a minor crisis of doubt—had I really heard God's call, could I cope with the academic study, were we right to have sold our home and moved to an apartment in Oxford? God knew my hopes and fears and gave me a text which I have treasured ever since that November day in 1978. Into my mind for no apparent reason came the text Isaiah 43:1–5:

> [1] But now, this is what the Lord says –
> he who created you, Jacob,
> he who formed you, Israel:
> 'Do not fear, for I have redeemed you;
> I have summoned you by name; you are mine.
> [2] When you pass through the waters,
> I will be with you;

and when you pass through the rivers,
they will not sweep over you.
When you walk through the fire,
you will not be burned;
the flames will not set you ablaze.
3 For I am the Lord your God,
the Holy One of Israel, your Saviour;
I give Egypt for your ransom,
Cush and Seba in your stead.
4 Since you are precious and honoured in my sight,
and because I love you,
I will give people in exchange for you,
nations in exchange for your life.
5 Do not be afraid, for I am with you.

I am grateful to God for this affirmation of my call, which sustained me through College and in the years of ministry which have followed.

God's call to ministry led to being the pastor of Highfield Baptist Church, Rushden, and ten years later to teaching at Regent's Park College, Oxford, and a further ten years later to becoming principal of the South Wales Baptist College, Cardiff. Throughout these ministries I have been aware of the need for relevance in sharing Good News, especially through preaching that engages with the lives that we all live away from the church services and church programmes. The two questions that students often hear me ask in regard to preaching express a little of what I mean. When we have our text for the sermon, I suggest that we ask the first important question: "What is the good news?" Then when we have our sermon completed and ready to deliver, we consider an even more important question: "So what?" Nice word, vicar, but so what?

Exploring practical and pastoral theology has focused on bringing life and faith together—bringing the problems and issues of life and work into the worship life of the church, and taking the challenge of faith into the workplace and home. This is the whole church living out our life as disciples of Christ.[4] For me it has

---

4. I have explored these topics in my text *Outside-In.*

included the dialogue between science and faith, and our call to care for creation, the environment. I believe that it is time for the church to stop playing games. I believe that Dave Tomlinson[5] was right and is still right to describe many churches as cozy clubs that proclaim middle-class conservative values and pass them off as Christianity. Many Christians are never challenged to see faith and worship encompassing the whole of life; there is a tendency for the church to be the particular club that some Christians attend in their spare time. For them it may represent an oasis from the tough and, sometimes, brutal world in which they spend the rest of their life. This is an unsatisfactory state of affairs for all concerned, and is far removed from the Christianity of the New Testament. My desire through teaching and ministry is to provide ways in which people inside and outside the church may think about the Bible and faith in the light of the issues that affect their daily living. But this involves a third conversion.

(c) Conversion to the World for Which Christ Died

Many Christians say that Jesus taught that we must be born again to enter the kingdom, but he also taught that we should sell all our possessions and give the money to the poor to enter the kingdom. Shane Claiborne observes that this is not very popular, but asks what it means to be born again into a family where our brothers and sisters are starving to death.[6] It is then that we realize that rebirth and redistribution (of creation's good gifts) are inextricably bound up in one another. When Gandhi was asked if he was a Christian his reply was: "Ask the poor. They will tell you who the Christians are." I may not be completely happy with this definition but it remains a challenge. Worship is the whole of life, as the apostle Paul reminds us:

> Therefore, I urge you, brothers and sisters, in view of God's mercy, to offer your bodies as a living sacrifice,

5. Tomlinson, *Post Evangelical*, 31–34.
6. Claiborne, *Irresistible*, 163.

holy and pleasing to God—this is true worship. **2** Do not conform to the pattern of this world, but be transformed by the renewing of your mind. Then you will be able to test and approve what God's will is—his good, pleasing and perfect will. (Rom 12:1–2)

Worship is not restricted to what happens in church. We must make all the connections between faith and life, and faith and work, and recognise that discipleship is full-time ministry for all Christians. Our Christian life involves every part of us—body, mind and soul, place and relationships—through every experience and connection with the world and throughout the whole of our life. Christ-like discipleship involves every part of our experience and existence in the world, not some fragment or scrap or occasional incident.

I remember speaking to a Christian speaker at a conference I attended about the differences between the reactions of people inside and outside the church—those who didn't attend church were more accepting of me as a person. His reflection was: "If the folk outside the church think you are too saintly and the people inside the church think of you as too worldly, you've probably got it about right!" To this I would add the comments of Mother Teresa of Calcutta (Kolkata) in an interview with Peter France after she had been awarded the Nobel Peace Prize in 1979. He commented that her ministry had not been very successful as there were still many poor and starving people living on the streets in Calcutta. Her answer was devastating in its simplicity and challenge: "We are called upon not to be successful, but to be faithful."

As the congregation of Highfield Baptist Church in Rushden grew from about thirty to over two hundred, the problems, tensions and expectations also grew, and we had more than a few difficult decisions to take. Once again I needed to be sure that we as a church were hearing God clearly and that I was discerning the right way ahead in my own ministry. One year when many such questions were the focus of my prayers, I was at *Spring Harvest*, Minehead in a Good Friday service. The speaker on that occasion handed out a hand-made nail to each of the two to three thousand people in the congregation together with a commitment card. We were invited to consider the cross and pray that God would reveal his will for us. Through those prayers I heard God ask me to commit myself to what God revealed for the church, without considering the personal cost. I wrote this down on the card and kept it in my Bible as church meetings and deacons' meetings struggled and argued over the mission of the church, often with criticism of the minister and elders. As I sought to work through these issues with love and patience, the affirmation that I had received from God on that Good Friday was both an assurance and a great comfort.

Many of the issues that we dealt with concerned the ways in which the church engaged with the community and world beyond the congregation. There were pastoral issues such as marrying divorced people or those who were cohabiting, there were worship issues involving music groups, hymns, songs, spiritual gifts, and the involvement of children in the communion service. There were political issues—I preached on Romans 13 at the induction service for the Mayor of Wellingborough (I was his chaplain), during the Poll Tax riots of 1990; and there was our response to "Live Aid" (1985) and the increasing inequality and injustice in the world. We also partnered Spurgeon's Childcare in the appointment of a family worker, based in the church, for ministry to the local community. Together with the congregation we explored the principle that a lived faith is Christ-centered and mission-orientated and cannot be divided into sacred and secular, evangelistic and social concern. This is the shared mission of the whole church.

I have been privileged, as I discussed earlier, to visit Brazil, Nicaragua, El Salvador and Nepal with BMS World Mission, the last mentioned while President of the Baptist Union of Great Britain. These visits convinced me of our call to be engaged in Christ's mission in and for the world. I experienced at first hand: the urgency of gospel evangelism in Brazil; the reality of poverty and political oppression in Central America; and the need to address environmental and development issues in agriculture and energy production in Nepal. More recently, I have helped Tearfund to explore the meaning of holistic mission, especially with regard to climate change.

I spent the last twenty-two years of my working life as a teacher of practical theology. This teaching revolved around theological reflection, helping students to think theologically. There are insights about self, God, and our relationship with God, which are demonstrated through our prayer life. Our prayers demonstrate what we know of God, how we view God, and our reflection on the circumstances we face. When we ask of a situation, "What does this say about God?" we are also asking "What does our belief about God lead us to think about the situation?" The experience enriches our understanding of God, and our understanding of God informs our reflection upon the experience, and how we should act in response. In my thinking, writing and speaking I am committed to an exploration of the relationship between science and faith, where issues such as the environment and climate change have helped me to understand more about holistic mission, asking: "How should we as Christians approach such key questions facing the world today?" We clearly must not ignore them.

The opportunities presented by my role as chaplain to Cardiff City Football Club for five years from 2009 to 2014, including promotion to, and immediate relegation from, the Premiership, brought me into another aspect of this mission. The stresses and strains of high-profile footballers' lives, the stress placed on the manager and coaches, the after match reflections of elation and pain. This is where the rubber of Christian ministry hits the road or the boot hits the leather—so to say.

The key questions for me are: what does this tell me about God? What does this tell me about the way that God works in the world? and What does it say about God's desire for my life?

One thing that I believe is paramount in our discipleship: the kingdom of God is central to Jesus' message and we need to understand that our calling is to be kingdom people, who are involved in building the kingdom. The church is not the kingdom, the kingdom is found where we are in Christ and Christ is in us. The post-resurrection church lives in the power of the Spirit (Eph

1:20; 3:14–21) and is called into God's redemptive activity (Rom 8:18–25). Christians have resurrection life now (John 11:25–26), which is eternal life (John 6:34–40; 10:10) or life in Christ (Rom 6:3,11; 8:1) or experience the presence of the kingdom in our midst (Luke 10:9, 11; 11:20; 17:21). We are called to live as kingdom people, who regularly pray "Thy Kingdom come, Thy will be done, on earth as in heaven." We need to adopt Jesus' agenda—to deny self, take up the cross, and follow (Mark 8:34). We are following Jesus and joining him in his mission of shaping the world, in the power of the Spirit. When the whole church demonstrates the reality of the kingdom's presence we will act as channels of freedom and justice for those who are enslaved, and we will offer real hope for change and freedom in Christ. We live within the hope that the gospel will influence lives by the activity of the Spirit; that Christians will be challenged to live sacrificial cross-shaped lives, which look to the needs of others. We live as those who know that the current reality of the world challenges our God-given responsibility toward our neighbors both local and global.

This is where I have now got to in my own understanding. What I am suggesting is a culture shift for the church. We will challenge the sacred-secular divide and discover the practice of whole-life discipleship, living as kingdom people; a whole life Gospel, in a whole life church, composed of whole life disciples: work, home, leisure, and street. This will be a church where anyone who changes employment will be commissioned by the church for their new sphere of mission. We are sent by Christ into whole life mission rather than leisure time mission. Worship is life; mission is being.

(d) And the Future?

There is the misguided view of growing older that seeks to keep old people "out of harm's way," by relieving them of stress and worry. But removing challenges and risks from people's lives runs the danger of making them feel useless and lacking meaning in life. To stay alert it is helpful to engage in physical and mental exercise, to stimulate creativity, and to maintain a healthy diet. I believe that my Uncle Emlyn presented a good example—he had gliding lessons for his eightieth birthday and continued to be active until his death at ninety-two years of age. It is therefore valuable to consider a conversion to the future that God is preparing for us.

When I was lecturing in geology, I spoke to a senior colleague about the research that I was doing, and about the ways in which my ideas were changing. He said to me, "If you can look back on research that you did five years ago and still be happy about it, then either you are brilliant or you've stagnated." Then, after a moment's thought, he looked at me and added, "and few are brilliant," with the implication that "John, you're not one of them." I would want to say similarly that if we can look back on our Christian lives five years ago and see no changes that have now taken place, no experiences from which we have learned, then either we are perfect or we have stagnated, and I would want to add that only One is perfect. My prayer at every stage in life is that of Richard of Chichester:

> O most merciful Redeemer, Friend and Brother,
> may I know Thee more clearly,
> love Thee more dearly,
> and follow Thee more nearly,
> day by day.[7]

I am still learning from students and the various preachers and teachers that I hear. A few years ago one of our lay preachers, Ann, was preaching on the Sunday after Easter having been given the passage that recounted Judas' suicide (such a helpful suggestion by the Senior Pastor!). One sentence in her sermon struck me forcibly and has been imprinted on my memory: "if only Judas had waited one more day!" There is a need to be patient and look for God's ways and timings—it's not all about me.

Recently through writing a reflection on retirement for the Baptist Union of Great Britain, I have begun to contemplate my own mortality. I am especially conscious of those of my own age who are very ill and have died in recent times. Aging is a natural

---

7. "Richard of Chichester," *Daily Prayers.*

and universal process and each one of us develops in a unique way, it is our individuality. Albert Jewell helpfully identifies the issues that face us as we grow older:

- The effects of aging
- The desire to make some sense of one's journey in life so far
- The need to discover new purpose for the years that remain
- Coming to terms with losses and bereavements and finding peace
- Changes in family dynamics and relationships between the generations
- Making the most of retirement
- If we move, where to live and where to go to church
- How to prepare for life's final transition[8]

The aging process follows common patterns but may be seen differently in each person—it is subjective. Our perception of age will depend on health and general well-being. Our genes set limits on longevity and dysfunctional genes can cause the early collapse of some organs. I believe that we should be encouraged to move away from the idea of aging being a process of decline and loss, and rather consider change, liberation, and opportunity.

Retirement is a good time for a life review, considering the choices and mistakes we have made in life so far, what unfinished business there may be and what the creative possibilities are for the next stage of our life. For most people who retire there are many healthy, active years ahead. Richard Rohr in his inspirational work, *Falling Upward*, says:

> In my opinion, this first-half-of-life task is no more than finding the starting gate. It is merely the warm-up act, not the full journey.[9] I believe that God gives us our soul, our deepest identity, our True Self, our unique blueprint . . . Our unique little bit of heaven is installed by

8. Jewell, *Grow Old*, 9–10.
9. Rohr, *Falling*, viii.

the Manufacturer within the product, at the beginning! We are given a span of years to discover it, to choose it, and to live our own destiny to the full . . . All we can give back and all God wants from any of us is to humbly and proudly return the product that we have been given— which is ourselves![10]

I have been much taken by Rohr's words that in the second half of life's journey one surprise is that the answer for loneliness is solitude—a time to reflect. Rohr believes that the first part of life is writing the text, and the second half is writing the commentary on the text. The second half of life is marked by holistic and contemplative thinking, which moves toward the *both-and* and away from the *either-or*.[11] We need to hear and see Jesus on his own terms. We are participants in the divine life of the Trinity. So he suggests that the first half of life is discovering the script, and the second half is actually writing it and owning it, or the first half of life is building the container and the second half is filling it. We build a foundation, we seek identity and survival, we look for success, but these are but the beginning—we have to take risks and move on. In church as in life we seek the comfortable and the settled. The demand for the perfect is the greatest enemy of the good. Goodness is a beautiful human concept that includes us all. "We grow spiritually much more by doing it wrong than by doing it right."[12] This includes failing and dying, which can be seen as good. Rohr speaks of love, death, suffering, God, and infinity as transrational experience—the opposite of rational is not always irrational.

When called by God into new situations, which may or may not be difficult and challenging, we are left to ask: How am I to live here? How am I to grow here? What am I to learn here? We need to learn to live in the context to which God calls us, not trying to chase either the experiences of the past nor trying to find an easy way out. Only then, says Jamieson, are we ready for the personal

10. Rohr, *Falling*, ix-x.
11. Rohr, *Falling*, 147.
12. Rohr, *Falling*, xxii.

and spiritual growth that God desires.[13] We can see this in Jesus' encounter with Peter on the beach in Galilee, where Peter is forgiven, and recommissioned to a sacrificial life (John 21). A new call, a second call, can come in and beyond failure. "To be called again is to be invited into a new depth of proximity of relationship with God."[14] In our failure lies the hope of new beginning. So Peter and the other disciples must go to meet Jesus in Galilee, where the bankruptcy of personal strength, integrity, and morality is named and the deeper grace of God is received, and "grace is based on reconciliation of relationship and love."[15] As we reflect upon our lives in older age this possibility is held out for us.

I should like to confidently believe the things that I wrote about old age, but there are always those nagging doubts and those anxious fears or regrets of not finishing or experiencing everything I want to do. We are all different, and our story and our experiences will be different from everyone else's. But our ultimate value is to be found in God; to be loved, accepted, forgiven and made new in Christ; drawn into an eternal relationship with God, which death cannot break.

James Woodward stresses that,

> We should not underestimate the spiritual and existential search for meaning that age can bring. The following questions: Who have I been? Who am I now? Who will I be? What will become of me? are very significant. These questions will no doubt generate a range of reflections resulting in meanings and interpretations that have a significant influence on the health and well-being of the older person. Life review, story-telling and story-sharing can offer a real potential for facilitating a definition of the self and exploring this in the light of the concept of "successful ageing."[16]

---

13. Jamieson, *Journeying*, 21.
14. Jamieson, *Journeying*, 89.
15. Jamieson, *Journeying*, 96.
16. Woodward, *Valuing*, 204.

His concluding suggestions are: be flexible; be ready to define yourself beyond work or the work role; discover your inner self; learn something new; take the opportunity to be someone different; get philosophical; and prepare for death.

As we grow older we don't desire superiority nor do we make knee-jerk reactions—we give more time to prayer and meditation, and we find that the beatitudes have more meaning for life than the ten commandments. We have a wider perspective and less boundaries. Rohr maintains that in the second half of life we do not have strong and final opinions about everything, every event, or most people, as much as we allow things and people to delight us, sadden us, and truly influence us. We no longer need to change or adjust other people to be happy ourselves. I find Rohr's suggestion helpful, that the end is planted in us at the beginning and it gnaws away at us until we get there freely and consciously. The Holy Spirit is our inner compass. This is our hope. True spirituality is the co-operation between God and the soul (Rom 8:28). In Christ we discover our true self. The true self knows that heaven is now and that its loss is hell now. The false self makes religion into an evacuation plan for the next world. The true self has learned to live with the big picture, with all of history—to be a part of the kingdom of God. God loves unconditionally and universally and calls us to do the same.

Helen Oppenheimer notes that we need courage because we need truth—truth that sometimes may be unpalatable and even what we most fear. Worry is of no help to us; "tomorrow's distress cannot be faced, bravely or otherwise, until tomorrow has become today."[17] Or as my good friend Kath Taylor said early on in my life: "God does not give you the grace for imagined troubles, but is there in the reality of life's pains and fears." We live by faith, as Oppenheimer says: "the Christian hope is not that we shall escape the worst, nor that it will not hurt, but that if we can find the courage to go through the worst there is resurrection on the other side."[18] As well as courage she believes that we need to foster companionship,

17. Oppenheimer, "Inner Resources," 41.
18. Oppenheimer, "Inner Resources," 43.

not only of our generation but also of those who are younger, and in a relationship of interdependence rather than dependence. There is also the Christian practice of the presence of God—faith that walks in the company of our maker. We often refer to those who share our life journey as companions. The origin of the word "companion" is to be found in the Latin words *cum* and *panus*, meaning "with bread." Our companions are those with whom we share our meals, with whom we break bread—sharing at the deepest levels.

My request to God for this stage in our lives is found in the serenity prayer, which my mother had on a card in her Bible, which I found after she had died:

> God, grant me the serenity to accept the things I cannot change,
> the courage to change the things I can,
> and *wisdom to know the difference*.[19]

In his conclusion Rohr says that most of us tend to think of the second half of life as largely about getting old, dealing with health issues, and letting go of our physical life, but the whole thesis of his book is exactly the opposite. "What looks like falling can largely be experienced as falling upward and onward, into a broader and deeper world, where the soul has found its fullness, is finally connected to the whole, and lives inside the Big Picture."[20]

I have found the writings of Rohr, Woodward, Jamieson, and Jewell of great comfort and challenge. I am continuing on my journey into God, who is my creator, and sustainer, who restores, redeems and renews. This is the God who has created the universe and has shared all our lives. As Jamieson maintains we are called to be there for people in the midst of their faith struggles, questions and doubts, providing resources, support and companionship for people seeking to contend with the difficult places of faith.[21] We need people with whom to travel, and who will help us to find God

---

19. An originally untitled prayer by the American theologian Reinhold Niebuhr (1892–1971).

20. Rohr, *Falling*, 153.

21. Jamieson, *Journeying*, 9.

in our desert places, and in God to find new depths of hope, faith and love. So we move on to explore the journey away from Emmaus.

4

Journeying Away from Emmaus

ONE OF MY STUDENTS at the South Wales Baptist College wrote about an experience she had while on placement at Argoed Baptist Church in the South Wales valleys.[1] Argoed Baptist Church has within its archives a recipe for an early type of yeasted, *bara brith*[2] dating from 1846. This rediscovered bread has been recreated by a congregation thrilled that they can lay claim to their own lightly fruited and spiced bread. The bread was used in a Palm Sunday communion service, and as the large loaf was shared the congregation were invited to think about the ingredients: the crushed grain denoting the crushed body of Jesus, spices bringing remembrance of the burial, water the symbol of life, vine fruits symbolizing both the life of the Jesus, the vine, and the cup of suffering. Finally, the action of yeast, unseen, working within the dough and bringing the loaf to life, symbolic of God's power at work—the

1. Taken from an unpublished MTh essay (Cardiff University 2011) written by Fran Bellingham, and used with permission. This work was subsequently published as "Reflections," 21–27.

2. *Bara brith*, sometimes known as "speckled bread" (the literal meaning of the Welsh), can be either a yeast bread enriched with dried fruit (similar to the Irish barmbrack) or something more like a fruitcake made with self-raising flour (no yeast). It is traditionally made with raisins, currants and candied peel.

miracle of bread-making, which led medieval society to term yeast as "Godisgood." As is often typical practice in Baptist churches, the congregation took very small pieces of the bread during the communion service, but after the service the members gathered round the remaining loaf, cutting slices and wrapping the bread in paper serviettes to take out and share with family, neighbours and friends. Fran Bellingham comments:

> This action speaks eloquently of the sharing of Christ with the whole community, the hospitality of the Lord's Supper extending beyond the walls of the church into the wider community.

Together and individually the members of Argoed Baptist Church are witnesses on the way of Jesus.

(a) Journeying with Others

The women have discovered the empty tomb, resulting in a mixture of fear, joy, confusion and disbelief (Mark 16:1–7). Following on from this Luke tells of another journey (24:13–35) recalling that Cleopas and his wife leave for home; behind them they have left those sad, tragic and traumatic events. On the journey to Emmaus their conversation is sorrowful. As they walk, a stranger joins them without their noticing. The stranger engages them in conversation about how they are feeling and why they are sad. Cleopas recounts his story of Jesus, after which he invites Jesus to stay at their home. As Jamieson remarks: "he stayed with them just long enough to help them rethink the illusion and rekindle the flame inside them;" just long enough for them to be "called to trust again, this time with a deeper and more inner knowing."[3] They have discovered that Jesus has gone ahead of them and that he does indeed meet with them on the road, even when they have failed to grasp the truth of the resurrection.

We take note of the pattern presented to us by Jesus on the road to Emmaus. This resurrection event provides a model for our

3. Jamieson, *Journeying,* 103.

involvement in the mission of Christ: walking with people and listening to their stories, drawing on our own experience of living the life that our friends and neighbors also live. We invite them to tell us what they understand about their life experiences; what they mean to them and for them. We walk with them and trust that what we know of Christ's loving presence will be seen in us and will give some sense to their lives. We make no judgements and listen and accept whatever is said; we offer hospitality as a way to really get to know and understand them. This approach affirms the need to listen to the stories of others and to live with the uncertainty of questions rather than simply offering answers. Peterson maintains that "it is the task of the Christian community to give witness and guidance in the living of life in a culture that is relentless in reducing, constricting, and enervating this life."[4] We believe that Christ is with us in the conversations and journeys we share. We recognise that we are all in different places on our journeys of faith, but nevertheless they are journeys empowered by the Holy Spirit and in the company of others.

An excellent appreciation of such engagement is found in the hymn *Brother, sister, let me serve you*, by Richard Gillard.[5] I first sang this at an ecumenical retreat for local church leaders, where we read Scripture together, prayed, worshipped and shared bread and wine. Some of the verses of this hymn sum up the spiritual intensity of that time we spent together, and serves as an example for our engagement with others on life's journey. A couple of lines from this song give an indication of its challenge: "We are pilgrims on a journey, and companions on the road;" "I will hold the Christ-light for you in the night-time of your fear;" "I will weep when you are weeping; when you laugh I'll laugh with you." We were invited to look into each other's eyes as we sang these words. This is risky fellowship; making ourselves vulnerable to others, but will nevertheless be fruitful for our own growth and prayerfully for those with whom we meet.

4. Peterson, *Christ Plays*, 3.

5. Psalms and Hymn Trust, *Baptist Praise and Worship*, No. 473.

Smith helpfully suggests that Christian spirituality develops as beliefs are examined in the light of our experience of relationship with God, with others, and with the wider world. It is in the Christian community that we share our stories, interact with each other, and interpret our experiences. Here is the place where we share our struggles, hopes, dreams, sorrow, mistakes, pain, discovering more of our relationship with God and others. She concludes that "storytelling, of course, is not simply a matter of relating an event—it is about seeking after truth that is beyond the story itself."[6] We may find this disturbing, but it nevertheless offers opportunities for our spiritual growth.

(b) Journeying in the Reality of Resurrection

After recognizing the risen Christ at the meal table, Cleopas and his wife rush back to Jerusalem to share their experience with the other disciples. The joy of the gospel is to be shared.

Worship is not restricted to what happens in church. We must make all the connections between faith and life, and faith and work—in fact our whole life journey—and recognise that discipleship is full-time ministry for all Christians. Our spiritual life is expressed in the way we, as individuals or groups, aim to deepen our experience of God. The kingdom of God is central to Jesus' message, and in Luke's understanding of discipleship the Kingdom is present with and in us—Jesus declares that the kingdom is near, in our midst, within us (Luke 10:9, 11; 11:20; 17:21). We need to adopt Jesus' agenda—to deny self, take up the cross, and follow. We join Jesus in his mission of shaping the world, in the power of the Spirit. We live cross-shaped lives in our God-given responsibility for our neighbors, local and global, praying that our lifestyle and values will influence others by the activity of the Spirit.

It is beyond the resurrection that the disciples, obedient to the call of God, find Jesus on the road—on their journey. Resurrection is the key to new possibilities in Christ, to the formation of

6. Smith, *Spirituality*, 33, 41–50.

Christian community, opening up the possibilities of redemption for human beings and for all creation, and for justice, liberation and hope.[7] Paul places the redemption of human beings in the context of the redemption of the whole creation which is powerfully expressed in the Paul's letter to the Romans (8:18–25). The resurrection has brought about a new reality, and the church is part of this new reality, the body of Christ, through which God encounters the world as saviour and liberator. So we are called to step out in faith, meet Jesus on the road, and be drawn into Christ's mission in and for the world, in the power of the Holy Spirit.

We are then led to ask, in what ways is the church engaged in the reality of such an invitation to mission? When we celebrate the Lord's Supper we are exploring our relationship with God through Christ, our relationship with each other in the presence of the Holy Spirit, and our relationship with the world, just as the congregation at Argoed Baptist Church discovered on that Palm Sunday when they shared the *bara brith*. Fiddes moves our understanding to a new depth, when he suggests that we share in the *perichoresis* (mutual indwelling) of the triune God.[8] In our identification of God as three-personed, Father, Son, and Holy Spirit, we are describing God in relationship, in community, and we emphasise that God is personal and welcomes participation. Through baptism "into the community in the name of the Trinity we are freshly defined as participants in the work and being of God."[9] The sacraments are a means of grace for healing and transformation, and for creating community. As we covenant together, we turn outward to the task of reconciliation that God has given us. Fiddes stresses that "the real presence of Christ is manifested in the community of the church, as it becomes more truly the body of Christ broken for the life of the world."[10]

Peterson similarly challenges that there is "no maturity in the spiritual life, no obedience in following Jesus, no wholeness

7. See Moltmann, *Jesus Christ*, 83.

8. Fiddes, *Participating*, 89, 281.

9. Peterson, *Christ Plays*, 306.

10. Fiddes, *Tracks*, 168.

in the Christian life apart from an immersion and embrace of community."[11] Our life is anticipated by the resurrection, and so the Christian life is not about us but about God. Peterson describes this relationship with God as "prepositional participation"—the prepositions that join us to God and God's action in us and in the world. We live "with," "in," and "for" God—we are participating in what God is doing and we do it in Christ's way.[12] Our celebration of the Lord's Supper encompasses all these aspects of encountering Christ and being drawn into his mission in and for the world.

So we journey with others, expressing resurrection life, and being drawn into the very being of God, who encounters, empowers and guides us through our Christian walk. But this walk will cover ground that is both rough and smooth.

(c) Living with Others in Vulnerability and with Integrity

In discussing L'Arche community Smith observes that "the picture is one of weakness and vulnerability . . . community is about diversity and difference as much as sameness or similarity. And also it is about the strength discovered in the weakness and suffering of the cross."[13] But the Christian church is not very good at owning suffering and failure. Yet walking with others and watching with them in their suffering allows us the privilege of absorbing some of their pain. We use the metaphors of "body," "fellowship," "koinonia," "communion," words that express relationship and community. The call to follow Christ is not a solitary pilgrimage but to follow in community with others.

As Jamieson maintains we are called to be there for people in the midst of their faith struggles, questions and doubts, providing resources, support and companionship for people seeking to

---

11. Peterson, *Christ Plays*, 226.

12. Peterson, *Christ Plays*, 335.

13. Smith, *Spirituality*, 73.

contend with the difficult places of faith.[14] We need people with whom to travel, and who will help us to find God in our desert places, and in God to find new depths of hope, faith and love.

Jamieson explores hope and trouble (Rom 5:2–5) and helpfully introduces the reader to Ricoeur's "knot of reality." This is a move to Ricoeur's second naïveté created through forming a knot of realities—"the reality of pain, suffering and despair that lies within and around us tied to the reality of a deep faith in God"—which brings hope in despair.[15] We can imagine a reef knot which bears all the stress that we place upon it; the realities of life being intimately intertwined with the promises and reality of God. The witness of the three men in the burning furnace fire (Dan 3:16–18) is an example of such faith: "If we are thrown into the blazing furnace, the God we serve is able to deliver us from it, and he will deliver us from Your Majesty's hand. But even if he does not, we want you to know, Your Majesty, that we will not serve your gods or worship the image of gold you have set up", or Job's testimony in his suffering: "I know that my redeemer lives" (Job 19:25–26). God promises to be present with us in the realities of life (Ps 23; Isa 43:1–5; Matt 28:20), and encourages us to hold onto hope in the face of uncertainty. We learn from Jeremiah (Jer 6:14; 8:11; 23:17; 28:1–17) that the false prophets promised hope without catastrophe, while God's prophets offer hope beyond catastrophe. Our hope is located in the promises and purposes of God, and this is a hope that allows us to make room for people's doubts and questions.

We have "seeker-sensitive" events, but surely now is the time to address the concerns of the church-leavers. The following provides a useful agenda, based on some of the ideas in Alan Jamieson's book, *A Churchless Faith*:

- Provide opportunities for people to explore, question and doubt. Open up a safe place where it is all right to say "prayer doesn't work;" "God has left me;" "I don't know whether I believe x or y or z."

14. Jamieson, *Journeying*, 9.
15. Jamieson, *Journeying*, 31.

- Explore a theology that speaks of journeying rather than having arrived. Present a "Pilgrim's Progress," where we can speak of failure and struggle, dark places and the absence of God.

- Build a supportive community which provides resources for people who have failed or who find themselves in the dark places. Be a community of nurture and spiritual direction.

- Be able to live with a variety of models of God and how God acts in the world. Be ready to admit that God is bigger than any one theological perspective.

- Develop a model of an honest Christian life, which emphasizes integrity rather than a legalistic treadmill of "oughts."

- Make space for the expression of emotions and intuitions, where images, dreams and feelings have a place.[16]

In our journeying with others we need to focus on what is really important. We have privatized sin with our emphasis on personal morality, especially in terms of sexual conduct, while our part in the major sins of injustice, oppression and poverty in the world are almost ignored. We make an enormous fuss about Dan Brown's blockbuster novel *The Da Vinci Code* and the film of the book, because it repeats in a fast paced, fictional story some common myths and heresies of the past, while we make little comment upon the arid commercialism and destructive racism that blights the lives of the young and old of our society. The prophetic voices that spoke out against slavery have been replaced by siren calls such as the one at the turn of the twenty-first century to boycott Disney World and Disney products because of their equal opportunity policy over the employment of gays and lesbians.

(d) Living Together

Our modern church, like the society in which it finds itself, seeks to exclude suffering. This leads to deception and game-playing. Also like society, the church has sought to exercise power and control,

16. Jamieson, *Churchless*, 145–51.

which is usually in the hands of white, male, relatively wealthy, intellectual, heterosexuals. The result is that others are excluded and move on. If they stay they are marginalized. As kingdom people we will be a community which reflects the life of Jesus; a community which reflects the life of Jesus will be a community of generosity and sharing, of friendship and belonging, of mission and identity, of freedom and risk-taking. As such it cannot but help stand out against the deeply held values of western culture. Such a community will recognise failure and the grace of God's forgiveness for all. We must face up to failure in ourselves, our attitudes, and actions. The Christian church should be a place where people fail, and are seen to fail, learn from their mistakes, and are forgiven. There is a problem of success-driven congregations in a success-driven society. Maria Boulding gives helpful encouragement:

> If we cannot endure failing and being weak, and being seen to fail and be weak, we are not yet in a position to love and be loved . . . Christ has gone down into the deepest places of our failure and claimed them as his own, and now there is no possible failure in our lives or our deaths that cannot be the place of meeting him and of greater openness to his work.[17]

We honestly face up to our own weaknesses and failures, and are ready to encourage others in love to live with their mistakes and failures.

Jamieson notes that "At various points on the journey of faith we too discover that God is not where we thought God would be and even, perhaps, who we thought God was."[18] At this point we must not try to deny such experiences, because they can be for us a genuine encounter with God and a step into deeper self awareness. In like manner Rohr urges us to see that faith is distorted when it is wedded to Western progress and ignores the tragic sense of life. Perfection belongs to Platonism. He challenges us with the observation that,

---

17. Boulding, *Gateway*, 12, 74, quoted in Pattison, *Critique*, 168.

18. Jamieson, *Journeying*, 105.

> God adjusts to the vagaries and the failures of the moment. This ability to adjust to human disorder and failure is named God's providence or compassion. *Every time God forgives us, God is saying that God's rules do not matter as much as the relationship that God wants to create with us.* Just the Biblical notion of absolute forgiveness, once experienced, should be enough to make us trust and seek and love God.[19]

He encourages us to learn and grow through tragedy and failure. Perhaps as churches we need to express a more realistic community, where we provide places for people to explore, question and doubt.

Such a demonstration of the kingdom lives within the hope that the gospel will influence lives by the activity of the Spirit of God. That it will transform the lifestyles of Christians and guide them to live sacrificially cross-shaped lives, which look to the needs of others. Our discipleship is a journey which includes: a longing, desire, and hope for a different world; waiting with those who suffer and grieve; the tension of the now and the not yet of our life in Christ—it is a keeping on keeping on as we follow where Christ leads and where Christ is in the midst. And all of this is in the presence and strength of the Spirit (Eph 1:19–20; 3:20–21), caught up in the *perichoresis* of the Trinity, the dance of the Father, Son and Holy Spirit, dancing ahead of us and sharing our journey.

Key to this is practicing whole-life discipleship, living as kingdom people. We understand the kingdom in terms of a whole life Gospel, through a whole life church, made up of whole life disciples. We can conclude that we are called by Christ into whole life mission rather than leisure time mission, where worship is life, and mission is being.

19. Rohr, *Falling*, 56–57.

5

Reflections on Journeying with Others

To be true disciples of Jesus we first encounter Jesus on our own journey of faith; we find community with others with whom we share this journey; we journey with others outside of our church community; we share pain and develop integrity. We consider our individual journey as a disciple of Christ, and go on to consider journeying with others.

a) Encountering Jesus: The Beginning of the Journey of Faith

There is a strong tradition of journey within the Christian faith, which has more recently been picked up by practical theologians as a motif to describe Christian discipleship. Journey and pilgrimage figure in much Christian literature, with accounts of journeys to sacred sites by Roman Catholics, and of the Christian life in Protestant writings. Chaucer's *Canterbury Tales* present the stories of pilgrims on their journey to Canterbury, while Baptist writer, John Bunyan's *Pilgrim's Progress* describes the journey of faith made by Christian, describing the places he visited and the people he encountered or who accompanied him on the journey.

There has been a growing interest in pilgrimage this century to places such as Santiago de Compostela, Galicia, north-west Spain. The BBC has broadcast three series of programmes covering pilgrimages to Santiago de Compostela, Rome, and Istanbul. The BBC Pilgrimage programme, *Pilgrimage: The Road to Rome*, first broadcast in 2019, followed a group of eight people of various faith backgrounds who walked together on part of the pilgrimage from Canterbury to Rome. They began on the Swiss-Italian border walking a couple of short sections before walking the whole of the last one hundred kilometers. The party was made up of actors Les Dennis (whose Catholic mother was rejected by the Church when giving birth out of wedlock) and Lesley Joseph (Jewish but doesn't strictly follow her faith), professional dancer Brendan Cole (a convinced atheist), comedians Stephen K Amos (from a Christian background but felt excluded as a homosexual) and Katy Brand (who was an evangelical Christian in her teens), Olympic long jump champion Greg Rutherford (a lapsed Jehovah's Witness), Irish Eurovision Song Contest winner Dana (a practising Roman Catholic) and television presenter Mehreen Baig (a practising Muslim). The conversations were honest and open as they each discussed their faith or lack of it on their journey to Rome, where they had a surprise audience with Pope Francis. It was the conversation with the Pope that underlines the importance of journeying with others and listening to people. The following is an extract from the Pope's words:

> "Life is a journey, whether you walk with or without faith, it is a human pilgrimage."
>
> Stephen Amos addressed the Pope and stated: "As a gay man I don't feel accepted."
>
> Pope Francis answered: "Giving more importance to the adjective rather than the noun is not good. We are all human beings and have dignity. It does not matter who you are or how you live your life, you do not lose your dignity. There are people who prefer to select or discard others because of the adjective. Such people do not have a human heart. Here, with you, I feel myself among brothers and sisters, and I have not asked any of

you what your faith or belief is, because you have a basic faith in humanity. For those of you who are believers, please pray for me. For those of you who do not believe, could you wish me a good journey so that I do not let anyone down."[1]

We meet and know lots of people: some are our close friends; some we may try to avoid; some make us happy; and some annoy us, but what I try to remind myself is that each of these human persons is someone for whom Christ has died. Each person has intrinsic value to God the creator of all life. We are all human beings and have dignity.

The motif of journey or pilgrimage helps us to move beyond the idea of a place to rest—a place to settle down into a comfortable life—and instead to explore the idea of being and becoming. Smith notes that "the emphasis on journey with others is a central theme in any exploration of Christian spirituality and has been taken up in both the Old and New Testaments—Israel in their journey to the promised land, the disciples following Jesus to Jerusalem, the post-resurrection encounter on the Emmaus Road, and the communal life of the early church."[2] All the time listening to God in order to obey, and meeting him where he is going. In this text I have made a journey of discovery as I have explored various scriptural texts and the views of a number of Christian authors, seeking to find out what it might mean to know Christ on the journey of discipleship.

The Gospel according to Mark comes to an abrupt end, the women go to the tomb of Jesus and find it empty, they are encountered by an angel, and run away in fear, telling no one what they have experienced.[3] The words of the angel challenge us to step out in faith and meet Jesus on our journey: "But go, tell his disciples and Peter, 'He is going ahead of you into Galilee. There you will see him, just as he told you'" (Mark 16:7). He is going ahead of

1. BBC2, "Road to Rome," April 2019.

2. Smith, *Spirituality*, 91.

3. For a closely worked discussion of Mark's ending of the Gospel see Hooker, *Endings*, 11–30.

you and you will meet him on the road. But this suspended ending leaves us uneasy, dissatisfied, wondering what happens next. In Mark's account the story of Jesus, his life, ministry, trial, and death ends abruptly. We are left hanging—like the end of an episode of any soap opera. But Mark's story ends here. We are frustrated, the story is only half told. Who had rolled the stone away? Who was the mysterious young man in white? Was his message about Jesus being raised from the dead true? Did the disciples go to Galilee and see him? Did they hear the message, when the women were too frightened to say anything? Ending with the women's fear and silence is a challenge to believe.

Human props are being knocked away—no facts, no eyewitnesses to Jesus alive. Just an empty tomb, the promise made by a young man, and the testimony of women. Throughout his account Mark challenges the reader to make up their own mind—is he or is he not the Messiah and Son of God? Mark is continuously challenging us to take the crucial step of faith for ourselves: Who do you say he is? (Mark 8:29–34). We want concrete proof of Jesus' resurrection, and that is precisely what Mark wants his readers to have. So Mark encourages the reader to supply the response of faith, because it is only those who believe and set off on the journey of faith who will meet the risen Lord.

The words "just as he told you" will force the disciples to think about all the things that Jesus taught them. He has gone before and they must follow, just as they did on the way to Jerusalem (Mark 10:32). But there they were afraid and amazed, because they were not yet fully prepared for discipleship. Now it is the women who are afraid and amazed. The story throughout the Gospel has been of the disciples' slowness to learn, which culminated in betrayal, denial, and running away. Now they are given a chance to begin again, just as he promised (Mark 14:28). For Peter this would have been especially poignant (Mark 14:29–31). The young man's proclamation is not only about resurrection, but also the offer of forgiveness and a new start for the disciples. The specific reference to Peter (Mark 16:7) points to an encounter with the risen Lord, such as that recorded by John (John 21:15–19).

As in the rest of his account of the Gospel, Mark challenges the reader to make up their own mind and to take the crucial step of faith. If they want to see the risen Lord they must respond in faith. They must go to Galilee—and if they obey this command they will see Jesus (Mark 16.7). This is similar to Jesus' own words recorded by Matthew: "Go . . . and surely I am with you . . ." (Matt 28:19–20) Resurrection is about new life—new life in those who have gone to meet Jesus. But this suspended ending leaves us mystified—wondering what happens next. Do we end with fear or faith? Those who seek Jesus will not find him in the tomb; they must look for him themselves and not rely on the evidence of others. Mark does not tell us whether the disciples actually obeyed and met the risen Lord. He expects us to set off on the journey to meet him—to finish the story for ourselves. As Hooker expresses it, "The ending Mark demands that *his readers* supply is the response of faith: it is only those who are prepared to believe and who set off on the journey of faith who will see the risen Lord."[4] It is this faith and this discipleship to which the gospel is drawing the reader, promising that all who set out in faith will encounter the risen Lord, and find forgiveness for past failure. The Emmaus road encounter expresses an even more encouraging picture that the risen Christ will encounter us even when we are not setting out on the road to meet him—when we are going home in despondency. It is the grace of God who meets us when and where he chooses. But nevertheless we are called to step out in faith.

Exploring this theme further, it is helpful to consider a much earlier call to step out in faith—at the very beginning of the call of the people of God in Genesis 12—the call of Abram.

We are told about Abram's family history, God's call and promises, and his subsequent response in the form of a journey. The call to journey begins in Ur. The trade route from Ur to Haran was used by many merchants and traders and in Haran the religious life was similar to that of Ur. Terah and his family would have been comfortable here, but Abram is called to go on. What does this call to go on feel like? The family have already travelled over

4. Hooker, *Endings*, 23.

six hundred miles from home; how much further will he travel? By the time he reaches the Negev it will be another five hundred miles or so. Abram is called not only to leave his home, but also to leave behind his family clan, all the familiar things of life and go; and he is seventy-five years old. Go where? Where I show you! says God. God knows the thoughts and feelings that must have been cascading through Abram's mind and he speaks directly to Abram with a four-fold promise of land, descendants, covenant, and blessing to the nations.

For Abram it is God who is the source of all success and good fortune. The command to go is outweighed by the promises, which are implied in the command. This is similar to the promise and invitation that the angel gives for the disciples in Mark 16:7. Abram's faith is expressed in trust and obedience. His knowledge of God is limited to a call and a promise; the place where God will reveal himself in a fuller way is not Haran, but in the unknown country of Canaan, five hundred miles from Haran, eleven hundred miles from home. The fuller revelation comes through the further separation. Just as the disciples experienced when they left their nets, business, family, and followed Jesus (Luke 5:1–11), and ultimately when they travelled to Galilee to meet the risen Christ. Abram travels from the north through to the centre and then on to the south of Canaan. He is claiming the ground for Yahweh, or more correctly declaring the truth that the land already belonged to Yahweh—that God was already there. The Lord appeared to him at Shechem, and he worshipped God at Bethel, yet Abram does not stop, he continues southward, and we leave Abram in the Negev, on the very southern border of the land, as God leads him into an unknown future, where he will fail and make mistakes.

This is a challenge to us who seek to be disciples on the way of Jesus, but for the moment let us continue to consider God's call and revelation in the Old Testament. In God's call to Abram we have a life shaped by God's promise, where God is providing new opportunities which can become historical events through human obedience. The promise of blessing is central to these verses; Abram receives God's blessing and is to be a blessing; he has an intimate relationship with God, who will bless those who Abram blesses. Wenham comments:

> The NT looks on the advent of Christ as ushering in the age in which all the nations will be blessed through Abraham (Acts 3:25; Gal 3:8). And his faith is held up as a model of God's dealings with all men[sic] (Rom 4; Gal 3); in particular his willingness to forsake his homeland is an example to us who should look for "the city . . . whose builder and maker is God" (Heb 11:8–10).[5]

Jamieson draws on the work of Paul Ricoeur, for whom the deconstruction of an old faith creates the space from which we can be "called again," realizing that being "called again" can never simply mean being called back to the faith we have left.[6] This can certainly be seen in the call of the disciples beyond the resurrection, and Jamieson observes that the call of God for Abram is to leave country and people and journey into an unknown desert. The call to leave comfort and security is God's. Jamieson, writing about Christians who being dissatisfied leave evangelical-charismatic churches, concludes that in journeying into a spiritual desert modern pilgrims are finding that God is already waiting in the desert, where they encounter him in new ways.[7]

When called by God into new situations, which may or may not be difficult and challenging, we are left to ask: How am I to live here? How am I to grow here? What am I to learn here? We need to learn to live in the context, to which God calls us not trying to chase either the experiences of the past or an easy way out. Through this we find the personal and spiritual growth that God desires for us. This is exemplified in Jesus' encounter with Cleopas and his wife as they trudge homeward after the crucifixion, in their spiritual desert. Where in their offer of hospitality to the stranger they find the revelation that Jesus has indeed gone ahead and met them on the road. We can see this in Jesus' encounter with Peter on the beach in Galilee, where Peter is forgiven, and recommissioned

5. Wenham, *Genesis*, 283.

6. Jamieson, *Journeying*, 10.

7. Jamieson, *Journeying*, 15.

to a sacrificial life (John 21)—a new call, a new relationship with God, can come in and beyond failure. In our failure lies the hope of new beginning. So Peter and the other disciples must go to meet Jesus in Galilee, where the bankruptcy of personal strength, integrity and morality is named and the deeper grace of God is received.

We step out in faith and begin the journey with the promise that the resurrected Christ has gone ahead of us, and we will meet him and receive the offer of forgiveness and new opportunities to serve and to follow. "But we are not of those who shrink back and are destroyed, but of those who believe and are saved" (Heb 10:39).

(b) Continuing on an Ever-Changing Journey

Meeting the risen Christ on the road is but the start of our journey. We might ask: How does my relationship with God, and my understanding of God develop? As a practical theologian I might pose a different question: What is the connection between the nature of theological reflection, the forms it takes, and the spiritual disciplines (traditions) on which it is based? For example we can consider theological reflection through meditative or contemplative prayer. There are insights about self, God, and our relationship with God, which are demonstrated through the prayers we write. This demonstrates a reflection on our understanding of God and of ourselves, for example John Baillie's *A Diary of Private Prayer*. There can be a common experience, which recognises our encounter with God: "Lord we don't know what to pray, but we know the one to whom we pray." This speaks with integrity of what we know of God, how we view God, and our reflection on the circumstances we face.

When we ask of a situation, "What does this say about God?" we are also asking "What does our belief about God lead us to think about the situation?" It is at this point that we begin to see the whole of life, our journey of discipleship: our thoughts, actions, and words as prayer and worship (Rom 12:1–2; 8:26). The experience enriches our understanding of God, and our understanding of God informs our reflection upon the experience, where God, the situation, and self are in a triangular relationship—with God at the apex of the triangle, the closer we bring both ourselves and the situation to God, the greater the possibility of understanding. These are the marks of being and becoming a disciple of Christ.

The objective check for our theological reflection comes through our current understanding or conception of God. But then we recognise that our theological reflection can modify or lead to changes in our understanding of God. However, this must be in harmony with Scripture, tradition, and prayer life. Such theological reflection has to have a credible theology behind it— but we recognise that a theological framework may differ from one person to another. For many, such a framework will be based on a living experience of God, which will be Gospel-centered and Christo-centric. Whereas from a more academically based theological standpoint, classical views of general revelation, special revelation, God, Trinity, the incarnation, and the atonement may be added.

On a personal level we may find it helpful to keep a spiritual journal, where we discover more about our understanding and experience of God and our self-understanding, through the relationship between me and what I write. By writing we impose a shape on the world—we construe the world, because the words we use are subjective. It is my world, because it is the world as I see and experience it. We reveal ourselves by the words we use; and if we do not question the words we use, we will never question how we view the world, and how we view God. We are writing about our experiences of meeting Christ on the road—always ahead of us.

Yet we need the presence of others on our journey, "where two or three come together together in my name" (Matt 18:20). Listening to each other's stories of our life journey helps us to recognize common turning points and features. When looking at our faith, our human formation and transformation, we should take seriously the fact that our adult identity and faith has been shaped by our earliest years and relationships. When we are open to God and open to others our faith grows and matures and our perception of how and where God is at work will broaden. We will find an increased range of people with whom we are able to share our journey of discipleship. We will be open to learning from people who do not share our theological position, or even our faith. We will discover new truths in new places and from people who differ from us in their life and faith experiences. We will find challenges, insights and new contexts for our stories, in the patterns within which other people's stories are told. In our faith communities we share our interpretations and experiences of the world and of living.

(c) Keeping a Spiritual Journal[8]

Let me begin with two events that I experienced in the town where I lived for the first fifteen years of this century.

My wife and I go to visit an elderly relative in a local nursing home. There are many residents—some in groups in the lounges, some in their rooms alone. We are aware of the sounds of music, televisions, nursing staff chatting, folding and sorting clothes and bedding, other visitors arriving and leaving with flowers, chocolates, biscuits, drinks. Mary is in her room on her own; she has just celebrated her ninety-second birthday. Her last two years have been spent in this nursing home following a fall in her own home. Her clothes are ill-fitting and stained by food, her eyes have red rims characteristic of age, her hearing is poor, she is fairly immobile, but cheerful and interested in family news. My feelings are of concern for Mary, sadness at her declining abilities, irritated by the lack of care shown by the nursing staff, but also understanding the criticism they get and frustration they feel—and I realise my selfish thought: when can we leave. But is there something else? Am I concerned about getting old? Do I fear ending my life in such a place?

Walking along the main shopping street in the town I see a young man waving his arms and shouting in the face of a young woman pushing a push chair with a young child seated in it. The

---

8. I am indebted to Revd Dr Jim Gordon, formerly Principal of the Scottish Baptist College for discussions we shared about journaling. Many of the ideas expressed in the following sections have their origin in those discussions.

woman is in tears, she is trying to place herself between the push chair and the man. All three of them are poorly dressed and the man smells of alcohol. Other people are passing by, laughing, chatting, carrying shopping bags, chatting to their children. I wonder what has happened in this relationship? Why do some people live such different lives? I feel pain and concern for the woman and the child. I think that I should be more thankful for my family life. I should make sure that I don't take my family for granted today. But is there more I should do? Was I too self-absorbed to have time to stop?

Two ordinary incidents that need further thought. The things that happen to us, around us, within us, register at different levels. There is the complex interaction of mind, emotion and spirituality, and the impact of the encounter on me, is determined by how attentive I am to my own inner life and to the life of others around me. So we examine those factors that affect our reflection and action.

(i) Emotion/Feeling

What Did I Feel?

We can consider the opposites of elation and sadness; reassurance and anxiety; clarity and confusion; peace and anger; openness and exclusion. We will each have our different pairings, but nevertheless we need an emotional scale or checklist.

Why Did I Feel It?

The connection between understanding what we experience now and what we have already experienced is a given of human life. Why I am angry with someone is partially answered by the history of the relationship I have with them, the incidents that are significant, the other circumstances of my life, and the impact of other relationships on this relationship. Each experience is colored by its context in my life, each relationship feels the impact of other life commitments to others who have different roles in our lives.

We need to understand this and know ourselves at each moment during our lives.

What Did I Do with How I Felt?

Suppress it or express it; escape it or examine it; prayer, conversation with others, write in journal; actions I could have taken or could still take. What is given and unchangeable in the situation; or what requires a change in me? Such self-questioning provides us with information on our own emotional climate, and is crucial in self-understanding.

(ii) Intellect/Thought

What did I think about? What questions were raised by the thought process—what did I think about what I felt; how did I feel about what I thought? Identifying feeling, clarifying thought, and disentangling feeling from thought is part of that instinctive desire to make sense of, to understand, and to discover meaning in what happens to us and around us.

iii) Images/Insights

Why do we choose certain images to describe experience? For example, she has a sunny disposition; like a spring day; as calm as a millpond; a maelstrom or stormy sea. Pictures, symbols, and images are shorthand for experiences. Is the image an insight or a distortion? What is the emotional tone of the image—reassuring, disturbing, evoking sadness or joy, a peaceable or angry spirit? Is the image a true and helpful assessment of the event? What color do we use to describe or reflect on an event or situation. "I feel blue;" "a red rage;" "green with envy." My wife was teaching a class of primary age children and invited them to draw a picture that expressed how they were feeling. Many of them drew rainbows and flowers, but one little boy produced a sheet of paper that was entirely black. He was in a dysfunctional family, and this picture did raise concerns for the teaching staff.

(iv) History/Circumstances

What is the story here? Each of us has a personal history, which often to a greater or lesser extent affects the ways in which we think and respond to people, events and situations. Often it is our teenage years that shape our thinking. So, when beginning a practical or pastoral theology course or coming together for Bible study with a group, I often work through an exercise outlining the world and church events of the previous sixty years, which helps us all to consider the events and cultural context that may have influenced our thinking. I start by asking each group member to tell me their age. If we agree that twelve to eighteen are the formative years in moving from child to adult, then a person's age will define the period of recent history within which he or she was growing up. So if someone is thirty-five years old in 2006, their formative years in the UK will have been the "Thatcher years" of market forces, individualism, and a growing materialism. In the church this would have been the period of renewal movements, church growth programmes, and Willow Creek. Whereas if someone were fifty-five years old in 2006, their formative years will have been similar to mine in the 1960s. This was a period marked by a growing liberalism, tolerance and togetherness. It was the time of "The Beatles," and of "Flower Power," and "free love." It was also a period of uncertainty, of "live for today," when the threat of nuclear war hung over the world. In the church this was the time of ecumenism, Vatican II, and the "Death of God" debate.

It is also important to think about where we grew up, our family background, and what our parents' occupations were. We recognize that there are local cultural differences, even within a small area. For example, my wife and I both grew up in South Wales in the 1960s, but Sheila grew up as the daughter of a coal miner in a small valley town, while, merely twenty miles away, I grew up as the son of a school teacher in the capital city, Cardiff.

These different backgrounds led to differing views over many areas of life. Church-going was the norm for almost everyone in my school; thirty-four out of the thirty-six in my class, when I was thirteen years old, went to church at least once per month, and the other two attended the Jewish synagogue! I grew up in a Christian home and my spiritual development was one of gradual nurture. We attended a Baptist church as a family, where both my parents were actively involved. It was a typical Welsh nonconformist church, where the meaning of the Bible was questioned, and its relationship with contemporary life explored, as discussed earlier.

In addition we would consider family background and circumstances, and questions about church experience and our journeys of faith. Those, for example, who grew up in a Christian home, worshipping in a fairly liturgical church, and gradually accepting the Christian faith for themselves some twenty years before will have a very different perception from someone who has come from outside the church, had a "Damascus Road experience" a couple of years ago, and has been worshipping in an independent charismatic church. Drawing a map of our personal journey of faith is helpful in understanding this aspect of our experience.

All of these are generalizations, but may serve to illustrate the way in which our experience will affect the way we perceive and learn. When running through this exercise in the Baptist Polytechnic University in Managua, Nicaragua, in 1995, I pointed out that someone who was twenty-five years old would have grown up with the Sandinista revolutionary government and the Contra War, whereas someone who was forty-five years old would have grown up under the Samosa dictatorship. These were two very different experiences. A similar exercise in 1996 with students at Georgetown College, Kentucky in the United States recognized the significance for the forty-five-year-olds of the presidency of J.F. Kennedy, Woodstock, the Civil Rights Movement, the Vietnam War, and for twenty-five-year-olds the later era of Presidents Regan and Bush Senior, in shaping opinion and outlook on life.

We recognize that new experiences will connect with old ones. We have filters that affect how we perceive reality, and influence greatly what we learn and do not learn. We have seen that important influences include our growing up, our culture, our education, our work experience, our pilgrimage of faith, our church experience, and our relationships. We will be conscious that all of these are likely to have an influence on our learning together and relationship with others.

Paramount for our understanding of each other will be an emphasis on the worth of each person and a recognition of the value of their experience of faith and life, whether or not we can identify with it. Time spent listening to people and their experiences through life will help us to understand how and why they react the way they do in various circumstances. How does this person's story enrich or impoverish my story? How do I interpret what happened?

(v) Humanity/Relationships

What is happening between people? There are the dynamics, relationships, influences and impacts of human interaction. There is both what we observe—the objective, and also the impact of those relationships on us—the subjective. We all need to be able to express how we feel and what we know or understand in a comfortable setting. This is best achieved between individuals or in small groups where mutual trust develops and each person feels confident and secure in expressing his or her thoughts. Here all are encouraged to tell of their own experience in their own words. Hope and Timmel are right when they reflect out of a third world context that, "Participation of people in shaping their own lives and to write their own history means they need to speak their own words—not the words of someone else."[9] They are right when they note that sharing information should not be confused with participation. Participation means dialogue which is based on people being able to share their perceptions and offer their opinions and ideas, and having opportunity to make decisions or recommendations. No

9. Hope and Timmel, *Training*, Book 2–3.

one has all the answers; no one is ignorant; everyone has experience; and we look for a mutual learning process. To do this we will need skill and sensitivity, especially as many (especially older) people will have grown up with a top-down direction of learning or imparting information through education, management, health service, and government. The result will be that many adults will be suspicious of this kind of discussion group and will, as a result, be slow to get involved. Frequently, this is due to a fear of embarrassment or the insecurity of being in an unfamiliar learning environment. It is therefore important that we shape groups where the members have the assurance of being accepted for who they are, where concerns and experiences are shared in ways that help members to get to know each other and grow in trust, and that each member is clear about the purpose for meeting together.

Maybe we should endeavour to take the attitude that I tried to instil with students in pastoral training sessions that there are no right or wrong answers when discussing our feelings, only answers. Along with other writers on adult learning, I recognize that adults have a wide experience and will have learnt a great deal from life.[10] They tend to learn quickly about things that are relevant to their lives, and their powers of observation and reasoning grow with age. However, we also need to be sensitive to the vulnerability that adults may have within a new learning environment, and recognize that they have a sense of personal dignity, which should be preserved. One way to get a group working together, and thinking about how the members can learn together, is to ask everyone to focus on something they have learned outside formal education, but which is important for their daily life. These should be things that they remember learning. Examples might include tying shoe laces, flying a kite, baking a cake, riding a bicycle, applying make-up, or driving a car. In each case a person might be asked: Why did you learn it? Who helped you learn it? What was the relationship between you and the person who helped you? What was the situation in which you learned it? In what way did you learn it? Can

---

10. See Daines, Daines, and Graham, *Adult Learning*; Hope and Timmel, *Training*, Book 1; Vella, *Learning to Listen*; Ward, *Lifelong Learning*.

you remember anything that made your learning easier or more difficult? The results are shared and will give clear insights into how we learn.

(vi) Theology/Spiritual Experience

Where was God in these events? What is ministry in these situations? Does my faith in Jesus have any relevance in these encounters in other people's lives? What does it mean to be Christ in this place and time? Are there clues here that give glimpses or hints of the Spirit's life-giving, life-enriching, life-transforming energy?

Our reflection that forms the basis of our spiritual journal is a process of owning our human experience through thoughtful evaluation of an encounter with the "other(s)" and "the Other."

There needs to be a dialogue between my experience and the shared experience of those who share my faith and relationship with Christ. My personal experience (contemporary and limited) is best interpreted, evaluated and corrected by the cumulative, historic, corporate experience of the Christian community. When the risen Christ had revealed himself to Cleopas and his wife they immediately set off for Jerusalem to share what they had experienced with the other disciples. It was here that not only was their story confirmed in Peter's experience of meeting the risen Christ but also in Jesus himself appearing to all of them gathered together.

We are never free to be the sole arbiters of truth (Eph 1:15–23; 3:14–19). We include our knowledge of the Trinity; of the love, value, and purpose of God for each individual, as evidenced by the cross; of creation and each human life in the image of God; of God's *kenosis*; of the empowering of the Spirit; and the insights of the church through such as: Augustine, Luther, Calvin, Newman, Spurgeon, Temple, Bell, Bonhoeffer, Moltmann, Luther King. What we learn of theology in all its diverse expressions, becomes a set of intellectual reference points to check, enrich, inform, illumine our experience.

vii) Dialogue of Experience with Tradition

Our dialogue with experience, what happens to us, has both inner and outer elements. Inner elements include thought, feeling, memory, attitudes, hopes, hang-ups, values. This is not objective, but is dangerously intimate and subjective. Our honesty and level of self-awareness will affect how we handle our own truth. We see this in the film *A Few Good Men*[11] with Tom Cruise as Lt. Daniel Kaffee; Jack Nicholson as Col. Nathan R. Jessep; and Demi Moore as Lt. Cdr. Joanne Galloway, where perception of and the interpretation/value of the truth is at the heart of the court case, which dominates the film. The story involves the arrest of two marines for assaulting and killing a fellow Marine of their unit, PFC William Santiago (Michael DeLorenzo). They claim that they were acting under orders. At the court-martial under cross-examination of other Marines from Guantanamo, it is established that "Code Reds" are standard at the base as a means of getting sloppy recruits to follow procedure, such as taking proper care of accommodation and equipment or completing exercises successfully. Santiago was clearly not up to the standards and yet was not subjected to a "Code Red" until the evening of his death. Galloway believes that Jessep, a tough commanding officer who is due to take up a post in national security, ordered the "Code Red" and that they have to get him to admit it. Kaffee asks if the men may have decided to take matters into their own hands. Jessep angrily rejects this stating that as front-line troops his men have to obey orders at all times without question. Jessep tries to come up with alternative explanations, which are torpedoed by Kaffee who demands to be told the truth. At this point Jessep explodes: "You can't handle the truth!" Because he defends his country in a forward area, Colonel Jessep does not see why Kaffee, who has never been on the front line, should even question his methods from "under the blanket of the very freedom I provide." Kaffee should either thank him for protecting his country and his way of life or take up a gun and do it himself. Kaffee suddenly begins a tirade of questioning,

---

11. *A Few Good Men*, directed by Rob Reiner, Columbia Pictures, 1992.

demanding that Jessep admit he ordered the "Code Red." In a fury, Jessep yells that he did, and is promptly arrested.

The film explores how each of the characters represented in the film discover the truth about themselves and the truth by which they live. It revolves around Jessep's comment/question about whether or not they, including Jessep himself, can handle the truth by which they seek to live. This film triggers thoughts of Jesus on trial before Pilate, where we find that Jesus declares his purpose is to exemplify the truth, a statement that leaves Pilate musing, "What is truth?" (John 18:37–38) Milne notes that in a world of illusion and unreality, Jesus offers the one true reality which is found in a relationship with God. Milne then wonders if Pilate's question indicated the wistful longing of a professional politician, "steeped in the daily compromises, the prudential balancing of forces, the application of ruthless power, the half-light world of grays and polka dots where people grope wearily for truth and the soul withers and dies."[12] Jesus might well have said, "You can't handle the truth." But for us truth is not found in a book or a creed but in a person; Jesus who said "I am the way, and the truth and the life" (John 14:6) and "In fact, the reason I was born and came into the world is to testify to the truth" (John 18:37).

Outer elements include people, places, objects and happenings—the circumstances and environment with which we interact. We need an awareness of the other. To pay attention is to see with the heart and the mind—to be like the poet who articulates the meaning and significance of what is seen. An entire spiritual discipline is founded on nurturing contemplative attentiveness as an attitude of love to God and others.

Our dialogue with tradition has four major elements:

- Scripture—the authoritative text of the Christian faith.

- History—the accumulated experience of the Christian church.

- Theology—analytic and synthetic reflection on Christian dogma.

12. Milne, *John*, 267.

- Pastoral Studies—appropriation to personal, contemporary Christian existence

Theological reflection brings our everyday experiences and the cumulative experience of our life story under the creative, clarifying, questioning of the truth and wisdom of the Christian tradition.

We can explore a case study. Consider the pastoral experience of responding to an emergency phone call to meet new parents at the baby care unit in the regional hospital, a little after midnight. Among the constituent elements of what we experience will be: the birth of our own children, if we have any; the emotional rollercoaster of the parents; the joy followed by anxiety; the radically feminine environment of the maternity unit; the fragility of the baby and the fatigue of the mother; the wires and tubes of the incubator; the awkwardness of being a non-family presence in an intimate place; cards and flowers; doctors and nurses; and deep concern. Added to this, the consultant takes you aside and tells you that there is no hope for the little boy, and asks if you would suggest to the parents that the machines be switched off.

- What theological reflections are provoked by such a visit?

- How does Christian faith shed light on what has happened?

- Is there food for thought; theological truth?

- What deeper realities are present in this specific context of birth and death?

- Does this deeply human event carry within it pictures of God, demonstrations of Christian doctrine—providence, creation, incarnation, costly life-giving love, trinitarian reality?

- Are there Scriptures which help us open this experience so as to perceive the reality and activity of God? (Nativity stories, Pss 23, 51, 139)

What would be the differences in our reflection if the baby were merely premature, very small, but nevertheless strong enough to survive and grow as a healthy child? Or, even more poignantly, if the baby were ours?

Any experience must be interrogated, enriched, and clarified by the truths and constraints of the Christian tradition. We recognize that our experience is not enough; that our insights are narrow and limited in relation to the accumulated wisdom and experience of the Christian tradition.

- When we enter our *experience* we encounter our *feelings*
- When we pay attention to those *feelings*, then *images* arise
- Considering and questioning those *images* may spark *insight*
- *Insight* leads, if we are willing, to *truth* and *action*.

How well do I see? Is my view point narrow? Take the case of the midnight visit to the baby care unit—there will be the standpoint of the mother, the father, the consultant, the nurse (who offered me the hospital Christening kit), and me the pastor. Beware the standpoint of religious certitude (Isa 43:16–19; John 9:35–41). Because of closed certainty, we miss the new gift available to us in our experience; and if we believe God meets us in our experience, we miss the gift of God, and perhaps God too.

Saul of Tarsus is the "patron saint of the closed mind"—absolutely certain—few things are more dangerous and damaging than a mindset hostile to those who are different from us. Saul's blindness was more than physical—it was moral, spiritual and relational—an example of those who look without seeing, who observe but misunderstand, in whose minds truth is eclipsed by prior held certainty. Saul's reliance on tradition, on his core convictions, was dangerous, violent, obsessive, and destructive. Only drastic confrontation and imposed blindness, forced a rethink, a new way of seeing, indeed a conversion (Acts 9:1–19). We all need to be converted from unexamined certitude and be treated for "plank in eye" blindness (Matt 7:3).

We also need to beware of a self-assurance that dismisses the truths of tradition. Tradition is the accumulated wisdom of our faith tradition; it is other people's experience, insight, discovery, mistakes, understanding, as those who seek to follow Christ. If I merely rely on my own experience and understanding, I will settle for limitation, constraint, and partiality where what is needed is expansive openness, freedom to explore, and a love of wholeness, for example in styles of worship, hymns and songs; translations of the Bible; inclusivity; the ministry of women; the use of liturgy and written prayers; art, music, symbol, and ritual. The Church of Christ and the whole Christian tradition is a corrective for our littleness of mind. They are a resource of spiritual experience which expands our mind.

(d) Guidelines for Keeping a Spiritual Journal[13]

What is a Journal? A journal can take a variety of forms.

It can be a factual narrative account; a record of a holiday or a travel experience, for example the works of Bill Bryson: *Notes from a Small Island* (A trip around Britain); *A Walk in the Woods* (a walk along the Appalachian Trail) or John Grisham's *A Painted House* (a semi-autobiographical story of a young boy growing up in Arkansas).

It might be a diary or recorded itinerary such as John Wesley's journal of his missionary and preaching activity, *The Journal of John Wesley*, or Edith Holden's *The Country Diary of an Edwardian Lady*.

There are spiritual diaries, for example George Fox's writing of his experience of being put in jail as a seditious and blasphemous influence. Such written down experiences become a resource for reflection, for deepening, appropriating, prolonging, revisiting, and so sustaining the experience. Fox speaks of the "inward light" or "inner light."[14] In our own time we might think of Nelson Mandela's *A Long Walk to Freedom*, or perhaps a book that I have found particularly helpful and challenging: Brian McLaren's *A New Kind of Christian*, which records, in a semi-autobiographical text, conversations with his daughter's science teacher.

13. Again I am indebted to Revd Dr Jim Gordon for discussions we shared about journals and journal writing.

14. Fox, *Journal*, 20–22, 339. See also Philadelphia Yearly Meeting of the Religious Society of Friends, "Light Within."

There is autobiography, which includes some of those mentioned above, to which we can add as examples: May Sarton, *A Journal of a Solitude*, a book which was originally written to help the author through depression, and explores the creative processes involved in her life as a writer; it was first published in 1973. Others we may find helpful are:

> Philip Toynbee, *Part of a Journey: an Autobiographical Journal 1977–79*, and *End of a Journey: an Autobiographical Journal 1979–81*

> Frederick Buechner, *Sacred Journey*; *Now and Then*; and *Telling Secrets*

> Henri Nouwen, *Spiritual Journals: Genesee*; *Gracias*; *Road to Daybreak*; and *Sabbath Journey*.

There are a variety of journals that people keep today. There are daily log books which record mainly a factual account with occasional reflection on significant events. This would be a diary, with descriptive commentary and minimal analysis. Increasingly today we see the use of blogs, which can be a frequent, chronological publication of personal thoughts and web links. A blog is often a mixture of what is happening in a person's life and what is happening on the web, a kind of hybrid diary/guide site, although there are as many unique types of blogs as there are people. People maintained blogs long before the term was coined, but the trend gained momentum with the introduction of automated published systems, most notably *Blogger* at blogger.com. Thousands of people use services such as *Blogger* to simplify and accelerate the publishing process.

Blogs are alternatively called *web logs* or *weblogs*. However, "blog" seems less likely to cause confusion, as "web log" can also mean a server's log files. Many modern church leaders publish regular blogs such as Brian McLaren and Rob Bell, and theologians such as Richard Rohr and N.T. Wright.

There are various kinds of spiritual journal:

- A telling of the story of our lives, with God as the other main character in the plot
- An account of our journey, with God, and with others, revealing movement and direction
- A record of conversations between self, God, and other significant people in our lives

Another form of spiritual journal is a reflective journal:

- A documentary of my way of life. A way of retaining my faith experience for future reference
- A self-critical tool which enhances the quality of my ministry through reflective practice
- A learning discipline which focuses on personal experience and vocational practice, and uses them as a basis for life-based learning

A reflective journal may have significant educational potential for the writer and may therefore be capable of assessment for educational purposes as well as being a valuable learning tool.

A reflective journal as a documentary on a person's life includes:

- Observing
- Recalling
- Reviewing
- Analyzing
- Organizing
- Articulating
- Paying attention to your personal story

It can also be a self-critical tool:

- Evaluating professional competence
- Increasing self-awareness
- Enabling self development

- Acknowledging gaps in our knowledge
- Building on strengths
- Increasing responsiveness

It is a learning discipline, the reflective journal can therefore aid professional development by incorporating lessons learned through reflection on experience. These can be developed through everyday practice, so that learning is incremental. Such reflection makes the connections between theological learning; pastoral practice; and personal experience.

The journal encourages an inquiring mindset which:

- Asks good questions arising from personal experience
- Identifies significant issues from pastoral practice for further thought
- Reveals an openness of mind to new truth and experience
- Takes initiatives in seeking further information and wider theological reflection
- Uses previous learning in integrating theological reflection, pastoral experience and personal response.

(e) The Journal as Life Writing

Life writing is an attempt to articulate and analyze experiences so that we better understand the life we are living before God. Describing the diaries of early Methodist women, Erickson states that:

> Diaries were a medium of interpersonal communication in which writers were their own interlocutors [involved in the conversation/interpreting their ideas to others], examining their attitudes and conduct as well as recording their blessings and shortcomings—in short describing and diagnosing the state of their spiritual health.[15]

15. Erickson, "Paying Attention," 92.

Writing was only part of the process; reading and re-reading enabled prolonged review, the tracing of narrative, comparisons of then with now, to measure progress. Concentration on inner feelings was a form of spiritual self-evaluation; and reflection on circumstances and situations a form of reflection on the activity of God in blessing and discipline. Such spiritual practice involves a work of our inner being.

In a reflective journal events are recorded in a way that contextualizes them, seeing them against the background of personal experience, pastoral practice and theological reflection. There must always be a dialogue between theology and practice/experience. If theology dictates what is valid, it becomes an imposed solution, for example Job's friends. Atkinson notes that Job's friends were uncomfortable when face to face with that which defied their theology. "They insisted on treating suffering only as a problem to be solved, rather than being willing to cope with the uncertainty of facing its mystery."[16] The closing chapters of the book of Job give us God's perspective, which both challenges human ignorance and encourages human understanding of God's faithfulness and care.

If experience is the foundation of our theology, then we have no objective truth outside of our condition that enables us to interpret it. It is through dialogue that we can pursue truth. What we are seeking is truth, deepening truth, new truth, clarifying truth, liberating truth, challenging truth.

The reflective journal is a process of paying attention. Every time we gain an insight into ourselves, others, or the purposes of God, we will be being called in new directions. Mutual accountability within a supportive community of love, helps to ensure honesty in facing our own truth. Conversations with a supervisor, for counselors, are to be understood in the same way.

A journal gives us the opportunity to listen to our life. We are the image of God, the child of God, only a little lower than the angels. Each one of us is a unique masterpiece, brought into existence by God (Pss 8; 139:13–16). Sometimes writing is the best way to listen to the reality of who we are, to explain to ourselves

16. Atkinson, *Job*, 16.

what happens in our lives, or to share with others those glimpses of truth that come out of our encounters with others. A reflective journal is a prayer book, a place where what we write is written by one who knows God is there, not only in the place where we are writing, but in the mind that thinks, in the heart that feels, in the will that is determined to notice, in that inner sense of vocation that urges us towards excellence in our service through growth in our gifting. Baillie's, *A Diary of Private Prayer* mentioned earlier is a helpful example.

Paying attention to our lives, in the presence of God, is to allow the Counselor, the Holy Spirit, to lead us into truth—to search us, search us out, find us, and help us to find ourselves.

We are learning by listening; we are listening to our lives and listening for God and to God, and gaining glimpses of grace. There are a variety of books that may help us.[17]

In my own faith journey I have kept journals at specific times, such as when I traveled to visit missionaries with BMS World Mission in Brazil, Central America and Nepal. These have helped me to communicate with others what I experienced and learned, but more importantly allowed me to express what I believed God had taught me. As a practical theologian I have constantly reflected on events and activities throughout the world, and these have been the focus of various blogs that I have written. I have also written reflections on films,[18] television programs and adverts, which address or raise theological issues. One example will suffice. I wrote this piece after the Boxing Day tsunami affecting Indonesia in 2004.

> If God is: all-powerful, all-loving, all-knowing, and ever ready to intervene, we have some difficult questions. How can God be both good and almighty when disasters occur? If we propose that God has the power to intervene in human affairs, we are left with the difficult theological question of why he didn't on December 26th, 2004.

17. Bass and Volf, *Practicing Theology*; Hughes, *God in All Things*; Clark, *When Faith is Not Enough*; Klug, *How to Keep a Spiritual Journal*; Neubauer, *The Complete Idiot's Guide to Journaling.*

18. Weaver, *Finding*, 175–91; and Weaver and Kreitzer, *Resources*, 231–307.

In 1755, an earthquake off the coast of Portugal caused a tsunami that destroyed much of the port of Lisbon and some sixty thousand people lost their lives. The Lisbon Earthquake is cited by some historians as a turning point for belief in a loving God. There were Christians at that time who saw this disaster as God's judgement on a sinful Lisbon. But why Lisbon rather than other cities, and what sort of God would do this?

We now know the structure of the Earth's crust; we can predict where earthquakes are likely to occur; and we know that the rocks and minerals, on which much of our industries are based are the result of crustal tectonics. We inhabit a dynamic planet in which earthquakes occur and people die. The Chief Rabbi, Jonathan Sacks said in the aftermath of the tsunami, that to wish the world was not dynamic is in essence to wish that we are not physical beings at all, knowing pleasure, achievement, freedom, creativity and love. We would be "God's computers, programmed to sing His praise." When faced with the goodness of God and the reality of suffering it is possible to adopt one of three philosophical positions: God wills or at least allows it; God is above all such things and is not concerned about them; or God is unable to prevent such things. The first position presents the picture of a punishing God. The second is a God who is indifferent to the sufferings of the world. The third, that God cannot prevent injustice and violence, takes us closer to the experience of the suffering peoples of the world. To say that God is almighty and God cannot prevent suffering only becomes a contradiction if God is placed outside the world. But when we recognise God present in the world, we understand that in love, God is involved with the oppressed, and through love, faces evil.

Different pictures of God in the Bible will help us; the God of love who: is self emptying; gives freedom; is crucified; suffers; and is vulnerable. Faced with the mystery of suffering we will need to hold onto the model of suffering love that we see displayed in the Cross of Christ, where we find the Creator suffering with and on behalf of the world. Our understanding of the cross helps us to locate God in the midst of evil and suffering. Fiddes acknowledges that no theological argument can justify the mountain of misery represented by Auschwitz, but notes that the *Shema* of Israel and the Lord's Prayer were prayed in Auschwitz, indicating something of God's presence there.[19] The same has been seen to be true in the midst of the tsunami disaster, where the different faith communities have each gathered for prayer. Fiddes argues that we can affirm that God is present in such extreme experiences as the one who suffers. This conviction that God suffers will also prevent the construction of any argument that God directly causes suffering, although God may allow suffering. This is part of an understanding that God freely accepts self-limitation for the sake of the freedom given to creation, and will challenge the way in which we understand God.

In his book *Love's Endeavour, Love's Expense*, Vanstone considers the tragedy at Aberfan in South Wales, 21st October, 1966, when a coal tip slid down onto a school and caused the deaths of over 150, mostly children.[20] Here God's step of creative risk led to disaster. Science and technology enabled coal to be mined; human greed seen in the demand for profit led to the siting of spoil heaps where they were; and the result, following freak weather conditions, was the suffering of the innocent. But Vanstone affirms that our faith is not in a creator who permits disaster from the top of the mountain, but rather in one who is at the foot of the mountain receiving the impact. His limitless love is evidenced in not abandoning people in their suffering but suffering with them. We attribute to God that authenticity of love that we recognise in Jesus Christ. Limitless love is not incompatible with the existence of evil and suffering in the world, since this is the consequence of the freedom that is given by such loving creativity. Following on from this, locating God in Indonesia amongst those who suffer points us to a God, to use Vanstone's image, in the pile of debris along the shoreline rather than at the top of the wave.

---

19. Fiddes, *Creative Suffering*, 31–33.

20. Vanstone, *Love's Endeavour*, 59, 65.

While suffering can sometimes enrich the character of the one who suffers and lead others to acts of compassion, confronted by the events of 26th December, 2004, even these benefits may not convince us that the risk of creating a free universe was justifiable. We can only think of God and such tragedies together if we affirm, with Fiddes, that God shares the consequences of his risk-taking love, and is able to transform the effects of evil and suffering.[21]

Through scientific research we can predict where and when disasters of this kind are likely to take place. So countries rich in resources and technology could counter such anticipated problems and avoid the worst effects if they accept the economic costs. But poorer countries cannot themselves take evasive action. Developed countries need to be willing to share their wealth, living space and expertise with others less advantaged. Thus, raising the moral question of the goodness of God also involves a moral issue for us.

In searching for God in the tsunami disaster I have wanted to affirm that we find God amongst those who suffer, seeking to bring about transformation and redemption. So perhaps the more appropriate question is not why did this happen? But what shall we do? We may not understand God but we can seek to imitate his love and care. Jon Sobrino in his book *The Principle of Mercy: Taking the Crucified People from the Cross*, believes that rich Western Christians find their salvation in their response to the suffering poor.[22] Suffering will always have a dimension of mystery, and no explanation, even one that finds God sharing the risk and pain of creation in the cross will suffice. But, like Job, all believers in God will finally bow before the utter mystery of the divine being, from which all things arise, and to which all things must finally return (Job 42:1–6).

The book of Job confronts us with failure, and with suffering for which there is no explanation. Atkinson in his book, *The Message of Job*, maintains that we have

21. Fiddes, *Past Event*, 209.
22. Sobrino, *Principle of Mercy*, 29, 30, 46.

to rethink our theology in the face of suffering and injustice. Job's friends were uncomfortable when face to face with that which defied their theology. They wanted to treat suffering only as a problem to be solved, rather than being willing to cope with the uncertainty of facing its mystery. The book of Job calls us to see things from a divine rather than a human perspective (Job 38 and 39), while Paul (Rom 8:28–39) encourages us to know that nothing can separate us from the love of God—that God is able to hold onto us through suffering, pain and death. In the end, Job is humbled in God's presence (Job 42:1–6). He has been caught up into the purposes of God, of which he knows nothing. He has to trust in the creator. As Christians we trust in God, who loves us and suffers with us and for us. We look to the death of Christ and see the lengths to which God's love will go. We are not promised freedom from suffering, nor do we know the mystery of God, but we are promised grace and hope (Rev 21:1–4), and called to a self-giving life that responds to the needs of others (Luke 10:25–37; Matt. 25:31–46).[23]

23. Weaver, "Tsunami."

6

Conclusion

THE EMMAUS ROAD ENCOUNTER from the perspective of Jesus is one of complete openness. He walks alongside; he listens; he observes the body language of the disciples; he engages with their story; their fears; their distress; their questions. He speaks about himself, the crucified and risen Messiah, and opens the Scriptures for them. There is no superiority, no criticism of a lack of faith or lack of knowledge and understanding. He gently leads them to a new place, where they will be able to perceive the revelation of Jesus alive, a truth that has been warming their hearts. They are clearly intrigued and invite him into their home, with a generosity of hospitality. He enters their home, their mealtime, their understanding, and their hearts. There is a *eureka* moment and he is gone, but they are transformed. Sadness is replaced by joy; confusion by enlightenment; and no doubt, with a fresh bounce in their step, they return to Jerusalem to share the good news.

For me or you as we make our journey through life do we experience the risen Christ walking with us? God is present with us through his Holy Spirit whether or not we perceive his presence. So there are two questions here for us: am I open to God, ready to know his presence, and hear his voice? and am I open to myself, my emotions, fears, and desires? I believe that Jesus does walk with us and is listening to, and aware of, our innermost thoughts and feelings. What is my body language saying?—downcast, despondent, joyful, hopeful, am I a "glass half full" or a "glass half empty" person; am I honest about myself, ready to admit my faults and my needs; do I express my joy and sadness to God in praise and prayer? I believe that Jesus does engage with us and will lead us to Scriptures that speak of eternal truths, and to other people who will accompany us. But we will need to invite him into our home, our inner life, and there he will reveal himself to us. As Jesus himself promised: "Anyone who loves me will obey my teaching. My Father will love them, and we will come to them and make our home with them" (John 14:23).

For others with whom we will share our life or whom we meet on life's road, this is a pattern for us to adopt as we share Good News, Christ's love, and the possibility of eternal salvation. Are we open to learn more of God's love and purposes from those with whom we worship. Are we sensitive to others, able to see how they are feeling through their body language and words or are we too caught up with our own concerns? Are we attuned to others, listening to what they say, both the words and the underlying "base line?" Are we able to follow the true observation that we have two ears and one tongue and give proportionate time to both? We know the gospel story and we know the words and truths to be discovered within, and it is these that we can share with those we meet. It is the promises and purposes of God revealed in Jesus' words and in the gospel story that can provide comfort and assurance, direction and truth for us and those we accompany. As noted earlier, I have often suggested to students in preaching classes, when you consider the Scripture ask yourself two questions: What is the good news? (the bad news is all too obvious in our lives and the world); and so what? (what is its relevance for us today).

Then we find that safe place where we can really get to know someone and their needs: we invite them into our home or accept their invitation into their home. I have despaired at student ministers who would tell me that they were not called to drink tea with old ladies. Because as I found through my ministry, it has only been through such events that I have learned about their life story and understood their needs. It has often been after an hour or more of tea drinking that I have discovered significant hurts or worries, and been able to offer real pastoral care. It is in these encounters that I have also discovered the spiritual depth of such older folk, hardly ever expressed in public meetings or worship, but nevertheless the foundation on which their lives are based.

In our journey toward and onward from Emmaus the two volume work of Luke gives us a clear framework:

- Cleopas and his wife are encountered by Jesus in the midst of their disillusionment, and he makes sense of how they are feeling (Luke 24:13–27)

- They open their home to Jesus and he reveals himself to them as their risen Saviour (Luke 24:28–32)

- They return to Jerusalem to share their testimony about Jesus with the other disciples (Luke 24:33)

- Their experience is confirmed by the experience of others. Experiences need to be checked and tested in the community of faith (Luke 24:34–35)

- Jesus appears to all the disciples and eats with them, teaching them, and gives them and us some guiding principles for the future of the gospel and for our discipleship: a biblical theology; an evangelistic programme; apostolic authority; and spiritual dynamic (Luke 24:36–49)

- After this Jesus ascends into heaven and instructs his disciples to wait in the city until they have been clothed with "power form on high" (Luke 24:49–53)

- Jesus' promise is fulfilled at Pentecost, when the disciples were empowered by the outpouring of the Holy Spirit and Peter preaches to the crowd in Jerusalem, and three thousand were added to the Church (Acts 2:1–41)

- But the road the Church travels is not smooth nor trouble free. There is persecution and Stephen is stoned to death and the disciples are scattered (Acts 6:8–8:3)

- One of those who is driven from Jerusalem is Philip. In Philip Luke shows us what it means to follow Jesus on the road. Philip, in the power of the Spirit, becomes Jesus for the Ethiopian eunuch on the road from Jerusalem to Gaza in the same way as Jesus himself had encountered Cleopas and his wife on the road to Emmaus. Philip answers the eunuch's question, explains the Scriptures and shares the truth about Jesus. The eunuch is baptised and Philip disappears from the scene (Acts 8:26–39)

We are now called to be Philips and Philippas ready and open to the leading of God's Spirit, and as Peter encourages us: "ready to give the reason for the hope that you have" (1 Pet 3:15).

Another Onward Journey

Over a period of ten months from September 2018 to July 2019 I had the privilege of sharing the last year of a fellow baptist minister's life. Bob Morris[1] was the Youth and Children's pastor at Cirencester Baptist Church; he was a founding member of the Children Youth and Families Round Table of the Baptist Union of Great Britain, and chaired the European Baptist Federation's Youth and Children's Committee. I had come to know him, his fervent commitment to Christ, his passionate concern for young people, and his wonderful sense of humour through working with him on the executive of the European Baptist Federation (EBF). Bob was taken ill at a meeting of the EBF Council, Lviv, Ukraine in September 2018 and for the next ten months underwent treatment for a brain tumour, and passed away suddenly on the 13th of July 2019, aged fifty.

---

1. I am grateful to Bob's widow Hilary for allowing me to reproduce the conversations printed here.

I shared a weekly email conversation with Bob assuring him and his family of my prayers. He had surgery in October, which was followed by radiotherapy and chemotherapy. The following are extracts from our email conversation. At the beginning of December Bob wrote:

> This week has been much the same in terms of treatments as I continue the radiotherapy and travel to the hospital in Cheltenham every day. It has been nice to catch up with people as they drive me. I am also continuing to take a chemotherapy tablet every morning and the good news is that I am still not having any of the side effects that could come with taking this drug. I do not feel sick or have any stomach problems so I am seeing this as good and an answer to prayer! Thanks to those of you who keep being in touch—we feel very supported and loved in so many ways.

In response, I wrote:

> It's really good to hear that you are surviving the radio and chemotherapy with little or no side effects. This is an answer to all our prayers. I've been reading a book this week that you might find encouraging, written by Andy Frost[2], the Director of Share Jesus International. In it he says some challenging and encouraging things. He maintains that in God's story, of which in Christ we are a part, we find that happiness is not the objective and that joy is the bi-product of a different agenda. This conclusion comes as a result of discovering that there is something beautiful about what it means for us to be a character in God's story. He calls us to give ourselves to God's story in trust and assurance of God's love and presence. I am sure that this is where you are and I pray that you will know the assurance of God's healing power and love.

Bob said, "I like that John—thanks!!!"

As we moved into the new year (2019) Bob wrote about a book he had found helpful by Craig Groeschel[3]:

2. Frost, *Long Story.*

3. Groeschel, *Hope in the Dark.*

Groeschel bases his book around one in the Bible written by an Old Testament Prophet called Habakkuk. There are just 3 short chapters and in the first Habakkuk is doubting, in the second he is waiting and in the third he is embracing the goodness of God. But here's the thing . . . .you cannot have a "chapter 3" type of faith until you've had a "chapter 1" type of question and a "chapter 2" type of waiting. This is because God can do more in your spiritual valley than He can on your mountaintop experience! Well, I've definitely had a "chapter 1 type of question"— "What's this tumour, radiotherapy and chemotherapy all about God?" I've definitely had some "Chapter 2 waiting" and I am still in that position really as I continue to undergo chemotherapy in the weeks to come. I am hopeful for some more "Chapter 3 type of faith!" I say "more" because I haven't lost my faith through this but have realised there is more to come with God and that is an exciting prospect!

I have walked with God enough "yesterdays" to trust him with all of my "tomorrows".

I will finish this part with a direct quote from Groeschel . . . *You can have hope in the dark because as you grow to know God, He will reveal even more of His love, His faithfulness and His grace. And over time you will realise, believe and embrace that even when life is difficult, God is still good!*

In response I commented:

Thank you for your reflection on the first part of Craig Groeschel's book. I am taken by his analysis of Habakkuk: doubting, waiting, embracing. There is a common OT theme of "How long O Lord?" into which Habakkuk fits. Your comment about "why not me?" was one that Sheila and I first heard from an older saint in Belper Baptist Church Derbyshire some 40 years ago. She was reacting to her daughter's sadness at the death of a baby in another church family. My reflection moved onto something that Sheila's grandmother used to say: "It is not what happens to you, it is what you do with what happens to you."

On a more theological theme, I remember reading from a theological work on suffering: What does the Lord want to say to me in this? What does the Lord want me to learn from this? What does the Lord want me to do in this situation? For myself, I would want the focus to be more specifically on God, and so the question might be better expressed: What am I learning about God in this? What am I learning about the way in which God works in the world in this? What can I learn about God's desire for my life in this?

To which he thanked me for my reflection and said: *Indeed— it's what we are learning and what God is teaching despite the circumstances!*

We continued our reflections on hope in the dark and I commented that answers to prayer in the valley of deepest despair is a common question for Christians of my acquaintance. Bob had written in further reflection on Groeschel's book:

> From our human perspective it can be strange to think that when God intervenes and finds me a parking space (*Don't pretend you've never prayed that prayer!*) but doesn't bring apparent healing to someone in their suffering—that he really doesn't care! Why would he answer one prayer that seems so much less important whilst at the same time allow our prayer and tears for healing and wholeness (our greater cry for help) to go unanswered? What is God trying to teach us in and through our suffering?

I continued with a reflection:

> However, when it comes to car park spaces, I remember a good Christian friend of ours, a professor of English Literature from Georgetown College, Kentucky, Ralph Curry, who used to say, on finding a space to park: "Thank you Norman!" When I asked him what this meant he said that Norman was Norman Vincent Peale, *The Power of Positive Thinking*—he thought it more appropriate than calling on God for a place to put his car. Mind you, I am aware of times when finding a parking space was

important in my ministry, and I did offer thanks to God not Norman!!

In answer to the question raised by *Hope in the Dark*, my experience has been of God's presence bringing a peace I did not expect, and the assurance of God's hand on the present and the future. I was in a Bible Study group yesterday morning, where we were discussing this very point. I testified to my own experience when my niece was killed in a car accident at ten years of age, our youngest daughter having emergency surgery at three months, and my mother's long battle with bowel and then liver cancer, and most recently my wife's four operations in hospital—God's presence and my personal trust that God is there beyond every circumstance. This has been my experience and the solid basis of my faith. I know that you are experiencing God's presence and peace, and I pray that you will continue to find trust and faith in God's promises and purposes.

Later in the year Bob was reflecting on a book by Viv Thomas,[4] noting that,

the author looks through the lens of the Biblical character of Daniel. As he was exiled in Babylon (certainly not his "First Choice") Thomas helps us to see that when things don't go as expected for Daniel then it can be an opportunity for good things to happen. Second choices can become places of grace, community and maturity if we chose to embrace life as it is! Daniel insists that second choice worlds are not places for failures but rather opportunities to demonstrate the reality of God and that places of second choice can become first class if we allow God to be at work in them! Daniel and his friends are heroic and inspirational and we can learn a lot about how they handled their "second choice" lives and not least the fact that they didn't deny their second choice worlds but tackled them head on and hand in hand with their God.

I can't deny that I would rather not be in this "second choice" place but if I am going to have to be in it

4. Thomas, *Second Choice*.

and to go through it then there must continue to be opportunities to develop and grow in faith and in character.

In response I reflected:

> With regard to "second choices"—the step of faith is that
> as for Daniel what appears to be a second choice is in
> fact God's first choice. This is, I believe, what living by
> faith is all about—Hebrews 11:1-3, or as I have quoted
> to you before, the assurance of Psalm 16:5 (GNB) "You
> Lord are all I have, you give me all I need, my future is
> in your hands."
>
> I pray that you will know this assurance this week.

In May in the middle of another period of chemotherapy Bob
wrote:

> Thank you for being with us—I have had a less event-
> ful week physically so that is good! However it has been
> tough in other ways (emotionally and spiritually) as a
> great friend younger than me left this earth after suc-
> cumbing to her own cancerous tumours—that is really
> hard for so many people to take—there are no words—
> just prayer and love and support for her loved ones at this
> time please.

I wrote encouraging Bob to continue in the hope that he expressed
of "waiting well," and encouraged him to follow in the prayers of
the psalmist, expressing his honest feelings to God in prayer.

> God is big enough to deal with all our anxiety and suf-
> fering, anger and doubts, when we his children express
> them to him. You are in my prayers daily, and with you I
> look for the 'new season' that God is preparing for you.

In his last reflection, a few weeks before his death, Bob wrote
about Moses' call to choose life (Deut 30:19-20).

> How exactly do we "choose life?" This is at the heart of
> "waiting well"—putting God first and walking in obe-
> dience—it isn't the easy option but it is definitely the
> correct one! It might look different for me than it does
> for you in a practical sense but obedience is obedience!

Choose it with me and pray we can keep on choosing it! And pray that our choices are life giving not life eroding or destructive!

CS Lewis wrote:[5] "A car is made to run on gasoline, and it would not run properly on anything else. Now God designed the human machine to run on himself. He himself is the fuel our spirits were designed to burn, or the food our spirits were designed to feed on. There is no other. That is why it is just no good asking God to make us happy in our own way without bothering about religion. God cannot give us a happiness and peace apart from himself, because it is not there. There is no such thing." Choosing life is a daily choice. Evaluate your recent choices: were they life-giving or life-eroding?

In reply I wrote:

> Well here we go again—God speaking to both of us along the same lines. I also use Scripture Union *Encounter with God* and was reading Deuteronomy 30, with its theme of *"choose* life." As it happened I was also beginning to think about a service I am taking in our local parish church this September, where the lectionary readings include Deuteronomy 30. I have attached the first draft of a sermon and prayers that I have prepared for that service, which you may find of interest/help, especially the prayers.

Bob responded that he particularly liked the prayers. Here are the prayers:

> Choose life.
> We pray for our families that each one may know the life and joy, peace and freedom that choosing to follow Jesus brings. This is the blessing and prosperity we long for.
> Lord in your mercy, *hear our prayer*
> Choose life.
> We pray for our community where many struggle with fear and anxiety and some with pain and bereavement. May each one who lives with the cloud of uncertainty

5. Lewis, *Mere Christianity.*

choose life in Christ who makes sense of our daily circumstances and brings healing and peace as his blessings for us.
Lord in your mercy, *hear our prayer*
Choose life.

We pray for our world where hatred and the lust for power reigns, where the innocent are the casualties of war and the vulnerable are left to starve. We pray that you would raise up leaders who will choose to live in your way, with the wisdom for good and just governance that is found in you. May they bring your prosperity and blessing to your world and your people.
Lord in your mercy, *hear our prayer*
Choose life.

We pray for those who offer your life in Christ to others, for our clergy team here in the Chellington benefice, for church leaders throughout the world, and for those who serve as missionaries and agents of transformation through the various missionary societies and aid agencies. May each one have the wisdom and the courage to challenge everyone you call them to serve with the choice of life and blessing that is only to be found in Christ.
Lord in your mercy, *hear our prayer*
And for our own lives this week—
Lord of the Journey:
the road ahead is as yet unseen,
yet the destination is clearly in sight.
You call us to follow the mysterious path.
The road ahead is a journey unknown,
yet you promise we will not travel alone.
You call us to tread the difficult path.
The road ahead is both tiring and long,
yet you lead us beside the still waters of rest.
You call us to walk the beautiful path.
The road ahead always rises to meet us,
with the light of Christ shining always before us.
You call us to follow your path.
So, we choose life and blessing through Jesus Christ our Lord. Amen[6]

6. The last fifteen lines of this prayer are based on a prayer written by Simon Woodman in Smith and Woodman, *Prayers of the People*, 104.

This was our final conversation in this world, yet my year in journeying with Bob was enriching, and an amazing privilege as we learned about God's love and presence on our journeys together.

Postscript

My journey toward and onward from Emmaus is now much closer to its conclusion than to its beginning. It has been a journey in the presence of my risen Savior, and in the company of many others, both saints and not-so-saintly. In the words of the Christian speaker and writer, the late Alan Redpath (1907–89), speaking at an ecumenical Bible Week in Rushden, Northamptonshire in the mid-nineteen eighties: "In football terms, I am now playing in extra-time." Like Redpath, in biblical terms of life expectancy, in my mid-seventies and beyond the "three score years and ten," I am also playing extra-time.

My journey has not been trouble free, nor have I always lived up to the expectations of my Christian faith as a disciple of Christ. I am ever ready to pray the familiar Christian prayer: "Lord, in your mercy forgive what we have been, help us to amend what we are, and direct what we shall be; that we may do justly, love mercy, and walk humbly with you, our God."[1]

My journey, and my account of it, may appear a little like the proverbial "curate's egg," which was not fresh, but good in parts. Nevertheless it has been a journey to and through the cross, a journey

1. Church of England, "B Penitence," B37.

of repentance, resurrection, renewal and restoration—and on more than one occasion. It has been a journey of hope as God promises to be present with us in the realities of life (Ps 23; Isa 43:1–5; Matt 28:20), and encourages us to hold onto hope in the face of uncertainty. We learn from both Amos and Jeremiah that the false prophets promised hope without catastrophe, while God's prophets offer hope beyond catastrophe. We can speak of the hope of judgement; that there is accountability for our lack of care of the poor and of the environment. Our hope is based on God and God's justice and grace, which is not thwarted by human sinfulness. In Romans 5:1–5 there is a link between hope and endurance; hope is the motivation to keep on going. We are faced with failures and crises in politics and public opinions, the situation for the poor in the developing world is reaching crisis proportions, and at the same time we see a return to popularism and nationalism in many countries.

Ultimate hope is in God and is eternal, while human hope is temporal and uncertain. As Christians we are called to a hopeful discipleship in the light of our ultimate hope in God's promises and purposes. We live as those who are created in the image of God and cooperate with God's transformative action in and for the world.

My one concluding testimony is that through the whole of my life thus far, I have known the grace of God, and it is in God who has accompanied me on the journey that I place my hope.

As the American novelist Herman Melville (1819–1891), brought up as a Dutch Reformed Protestant and famous for his novel *Moby-Dick* (1851), wrote:

Life's a journey that's homeward bound.[2]

---

2. Melville, *White-Jacket*, 374.

Bibliography

Atkinson, David. *The Message of Job*. The Bible Speaks Today. Leicester: Inter Varsity Press, 1991

Baillie, Donald M. *The Theology of the Sacraments*. London: Faber & Faber, 1957

Baillie, John. *A Diary of Private Prayer*. New York: Simon & Schuster, 2014

Bass, Dorothy, and Miroslav Volf. *Practising Theology: Beliefs and Practices in Christian Life*. Grand Rapids: Eerdmans, 2001

BBC2. "Pilgrimage: The Road to Rome." April, 2019. https://www.bbc.co.uk/programmes/m0003wws.

Bellingham, Fran. "Reflections: Eucharistic meals." *Baptist Ministers' Journal* 317 (2013) 21–27.

Boulding, Maria. *Gateway to Hope*. London: Collins/Fount, 1985.

Caird, G. B. *The Gospel of Saint Luke*. The Pelican New Testament Commentaries. London: Penguin, 1977.

Carroll, John T. *Luke: A Commentary*. Louisville: Westminster John Knox, 2012.

Church of England. "B Penitence." https://www.churchofengland.org/prayer-and-worship/worship-texts-and-resources/common-worship/common-material/new-patterns-12.

Claiborne, Shane. *The Irresistible Revolution: Living as an Ordinary Radical*, Grand Rapids: Zondervan, 2006.

Clark, Kelly James. *When Faith is Not Enough*. Grand Rapids: Eerdmans, 1997.

Cross, F. L., and E. A. Livingstone. *The Oxford Dictionary of the Christian Church*. Oxford: Oxford University Press, 1983.

Daines, John, Carolyn Daines, and Brian Graham. *Adult Learning, Adult Teaching*. Nottingham: University of Nottingham, 1993.

Edwards, James R. *The Gospel According to Luke*. Pillar New Testament Commentary. Grand Rapids: Eerdmans, 2015.

Bibliography

Encyclopedia Britannica Online, s.v. "Nikolaus Ludwig, count von Zinzendorf." https://www.britannica.com/biography/Nikolaus-Ludwig-Graf-von-Zinzendorf.

Erickson, J. Q. "Paying Attention: Holiness in the Life Writings of Early Methodist Women." In *Embodied Holiness*, edited by S. Powell and M. Lodahl, 89–114. Downers Grove: InterVarsity, 1999.

Fiddes, Paul S. *The Creative Suffering of God*. Oxford: Clarendon, 1988

——. *Past Event and Present Salvation: The Christian Idea of Atonement*. London: Darton Longman & Todd, 1989.

——. *Participating in God: A Pastoral Doctrine of the Trinity*. London: Darton Longman & Todd, 2000.

——. *Tracks and Traces. Baptist Identity in Church and Theology*. Carlisle: Paternoster, 2003.

Fox, George. *The Journal of George Fox*. Revised by Norman Penney. London: J. M. Dent, 1924, 1940.

Green, Joel B. *The Gospel of Luke*. The New International Commentary on the New Testament. Grand Rapids: Eerdmans, 1997.

Groeschel, Craig. *Hope in the Dark. Believing God is good when life is not*. Grand Rapids: Zondervan, 2018.

Groome, Thomas H. *Christian Religious Education: Sharing our Story and Vision*. San Francisco: Harper & Row, 1980.

Hooker, Morna D. *Endings. Invitations to Discipleship*. London: SCM, 2003.

Hope, Anne and Sally Timmel. *Training for Transformation. A Handbook for Community Workers*. Harare: Mambo, 1984.

Hughes, Gerard W. *God in All Things*. London: Hodder & Stoughton, 2003.

Jamieson, Alan. *A Churchless Faith. Faith Journeys beyond the Churches*. London: SPCK, 2002.

——. *Journeying in Faith: In and Beyond the tough Places*. London: SPCK, 2004.

Jewell, Albert. *Grow old along with me*. Birmingham: National Christian Education Council, 2000.

Jump, Phil, and John Weaver. *Love:Work. Reflections and Prayers for a World at Work*. London: Darton Longman & Todd, 2021.

Klug, Ron. *How to Keep a Spiritual Journal*. Minneapolis: Augsburg, 2002.

Kreider, Eleanor. *Communion Shapes Character*. Scottdale: Herald, 1997.

Lewis, C. S. *Mere Christianity,* London: Collins, 2012.

Lieu, Judith. *The Gospel of Luke*. Eugene, Oregon: Wipf & Stock, 1997.

Marshall, I. Howard. *The Gospel of Luke. A Commentary on the Greek Text*. Exeter: Paternoster, 1978.

McLaren, Brian D. *Everything Must Change. Jesus, Global Crises, and a Revolution of Hope*. Nashville: Thomas Nelson, 2007.

McClendon, James Wm. Jr. *Biography as Theology*. Philadelphia: Trinity, 1990.

Melville, Herman. *White-Jacket*. New York: A.L. Burt Company, 1850.

Milne, Bruce. *The Message of John*. The Bible Speaks Today. Leicester: Inter Varsity, 1993.

Bibliography

Moltmann, Jürgen. *Jesus Christ for Today's World*. London: SCM, 1995.

Morris, Leon. *Luke*. Tyndale New Testament Commentaries. Nottingham: Inter Varsity, 2008.

Moule, C. F. D. *The Sacrifice of Christ*. London: Hodder & Stoughton, 1956.

Neubauer, Joan R. *The Complete Idiot's Guide to Journaling*. New York: Penguin, 2000.

Nolland, John. *Luke 18:35—24:53*. Word Bible Commentary 35C. Grand Rapids: Zondervan, 2018.

Oppenheimer, Helen. "Inner Resources for Growing Older." In *Spirituality and Ageing*, edited by Albert Jewell, 39–47. London: Jessica Kingsley, 1999.

Paisley, Ian. "Tributes: Bill Clinton, John Hume and Ian Paisley Jnr among those paying tribute to Martin McGuinness." *Irish News*. https://www.irishnews.com/news/northernirelandnews/2017/03/21/news/tributes-arlene-foster-says-history-would-record-differing-views-on-martin-mcguinness-971349/.

Pattison, Stephen. *Critique of Pastoral Care*. London: SPCK, 1993.

Peterson, Eugene H. *Christ Plays in Ten Thousand Places. A Conversation in Spiritual Theology*. London: Hodder & Stoughton, 2005.

———. *The Message Study Bible*. Colorado Springs: Tyndale House, 2012.

Philadelphia Yearly Meeting of the Religious Society of Friends. "The Light Within." https://www.pym.org/faith-and-practice/experience-and-faith/the-light-within/.

Psalms and Hymn Trust. *Baptist Praise and Worship*. Oxford: Oxford University Press, 1991.

"Richard of Chichester." *Daily Prayers*. https://www.daily-prayers.org/angels-and-saints/prayers-of-saint-richard-of-chichester/.

Rohr, Richard. *Falling Upward. A Spirituality for the Two Halves of Life*. London: SPCK, 2012.

Smith, Karen E. *Christian Spirituality*. SCM Core Text. London: SCM, 2007.

Sobrino, Jon. *The Principle of Mercy: Taking the Crucified People from the Cross*. New York: Orbis, 1994.

Talbert, Charles. *Reading Luke. A Literary and Theological Commentary on the Third Gospel*. New York: Crossroad, 1982.

Thomas, Viv. *Second Choice, Embracing Life as It Is*. London: Formation Global, 2018.

Tomlinson, Dave. *Post Evangelical*. London: Triangle, SPCK, 1995.

Vanstone, W. H. *Love's Endeavour, Love's Expense*. London: Darton, Longman & Todd, 1977.

Vella, Jane. *Learning to Listen, Learning to Teach: The Power of Dialogue in Educating Adults*. San Francisco: Jossey-Bass, 1994.

Ward, Frances. *Lifelong Learning: Theological Education and Supervision*. London: SCM, 2005.

Ward, Reginald and Richard P. Heitzenrater, eds. *The Works of John Wesley: Journals and Diaries*. Vols 18–24. Nashville: Abingdon, 1988–2003.

Bibliography

Weaver, John. "Tsunami (26th December, 2004)—a reflection." *Baptist Times* January 2005.

———. "Finding God in the Holocaust: *Schindler's List.*" In *Flickering Images: Theology and Film in Dialogue,* edited by Anthony J Clarke & Paul S Fiddes, 175–91. Oxford: Regent's Park College, 2005.

———. *Outside-In: Theological Reflections on Life.* Oxford: Regent's Park College, 2006

———, "Spirituality in Everyday Life: the View from the Table." In *Under the Rule of Christ: Dimensions of Baptist Spirituality,* edited by Paul S. Fiddes, 135–67.Oxford: Regent's Park College, 2008.

———. *Christianity and Science: SCM Core Text.* London: SCM, 2010.

Weaver, John, and Larry Kreitzer. "Part Three: Resources." In *Flickering Images. Theology and Film in Dialogue,* edited by Anthony J Clarke and Paul S Fiddes, 229–307.Oxford: Regent's Park College, 2005.

Wenham, Gordon J. *Genesis 1–15.* Word Bible Commentary. Waco, TX: Word, 1987.

Wilcock, Michael. *The Message of Luke. The Saviour of the World.* The Bible Speaks Today. Leicester: InterVarsity, 1979.

Woodman, Simon P. In *Prayers of the People,* edited by Karen E. Smith and Simon P. Woodman, 104. Oxford: Regent's Park College, 2011.

Wright, N. T. *Luke for Everyone.* London: SPCK, 2004.